WHY WOULD THEY SAY IT?

(IF IT WASN'T TRUE)

KEN HUDNALL

WHY WOULD THEY SAY IT?

COPYRIGHT © 2017 KEN HUDNALL

PRUNE DANISH PRESS

http://www.kenhudnall.com

FIRST EDITION

Printed in the United States of America

PROLOGUE

Before I tell my story, there are a few basic points of law that I wish to have viewed as the backdrop to everything that happened. Though these points of law are taught in every law school in the country, apparently judges forget them, or really don't care anymore once they become members of the anointed. As you read these pages you will see that State Attorney Generals, Governors, Mayors, attorneys, state and federal judges committed serious crimes, but they are apparently above the laws that the rest of us have to obey. Now let's look at a little Law 101:

FIRST: This is a country of laws. Our legal system is allegedly based upon the United States Constitution and the Bill of Rights. Our judges and politicians give lip service to this, but at the same time, laugh up their sleeves that the rest of us are so stupid as to believe it.

SECOND: Incorporated into the U.S. Constitution in both the Fifth as well as the 14th Amendments to this documents is something called the Right to Due Process of Law[1].

---

[1] Due process in the taking of property by any arm of the State is a civil right guaranteed by Section One of the 14th Amendment of the

THIRD: The U.S. Supreme Court has held:

"The assertion of federal rights, when plainly and reasonably made, is not to be defeated under the name of local practice." **Davis v Wechsler**, 263 U.S. 22, 24 (1923)

"Where rights secured by the Constitution are involved, there can be no rule making or legislation which would abrogate them." **Miranda v Arizona**, 384 U.S. 426, 491 (1966).

FOURTH: The right to practice law has been determined by the U.S. Supreme Court to be property. In **Schwarz v. Board of Bar Examiners** and **Konigsberg v. State Bar of California**[2], the U.S. Supreme Court very clearly stated, the right to practice law is a property right within the due process and equal protection provisions of the Fourteenth Amendment of the U.S. Constitution of the United States.

Nowhere in the terms of the Fourteenth Amendment does it exclude American citizens, the disabled or veterans from equal protection of the law as I have been excluded.

Constitution. Conspiracy to deny due process is a federal felony prosecutable under 18 USC 241. Denial of due process under color of law is a federal misdemeanor under 18 USC 242.

[2] **Schwarz v. Board of Bar Examiners**, 353 U.S. 232, 77 S.Ct. 752, 1 L.Ed 2d 796 and **Konigsberg v. State Bar of California**, 353 U.S. 252, 77 S.Ct. 722, 1 L.Ed. 2d 810.

and it cannot be taken from me without a notice of charges and the right to be heard before a fair tribunal[3].

FIFTH: The United States Supreme Court has determined that the right to practice law is a privilege or immunity under the Privileges and Immunity Clause of the United States Constitution[4].

SIXTH: A Court's jurisdiction or power must be established by some legal document. In the Case of the Court (I say that laughingly) that illegally took my right to practice law, it was the Supreme Court of the State of Georgia which, as established by the State Constitution has only appellate jurisdiction. It could not make an original decision, had no power to serve me with process to appear in court or empanel a jury. I was never allowed to be heard,

---

[3] In **Bradley v. Fisher**, 60 U.S. 335, 20 L.Ed 645 (1871) the high court held: "In order to revoke or suspend the license of an attorney, the law requires that there should be an accusation and charges, a notice and a day in court, and it cannot be done summarily by order of the court. The law makes no difference between an attorney and other holding office during good behavior and other vested rights to be taken away by "due process of law," and requires in every case or proceeding to take away such an office, right or franchise, that the party shall have notice and opportunity to be heard, before the Court can acquire jurisdiction to adjudicate and that *jurisdiction is limited to the exercise of a legal discretion by a court and does not include arbitrary acts of a judge*."
[4] In the case cited as **Supreme Court of New Hampshire v. Piper**, 470 U.S. 274, 105 S. Ct. 1272, 84 L. Ed. 2d 205, 1985 U.S, the U.S. Supreme Court clearly stated the right to practice law is a "fundamental right" and therefore protected by the Fourteenth Amendment's Privileges and Immunities Clause of the U.S Constitution.

in fact the court refused to allow me to be heard as shown in the exhibits.

SEVENTH: A court is thought of as having the job of ruling according to law. In my case, the court allowed collusion and bribery to be committed by at least two State Bars, lying by attorneys, the ignoring of properly issued subpoenas and then went out of its way to cover-up the acts of those who violated my right to due process of law. The governor of New Mexico turned a blind eye to corruption in the judiciary in her state.

EIGHTH: The Director of the Federal Bureau of Investigation is REQUIRED by 28 CFR 0.85 to investigate violations of 18 USC 241 and 18 USC 242.

THE F.B.I. HAS ALWAYS TURNED ITS BACK ON ME – TOO MANY GOOD DEMOCRATS MIGHT GET HURT.

Why would so many, break the law in regard to my case - to protect the income stream of ill-gotten gains that was a recognized "perk". Justice de damned. My rights were taken illegally, everything else is cover-up. Against the legal background as outlined, read my story, if you dare!

Contents

CHAPTER ONE
HOW THIS CAME TO BE

As I write these words, the world is in a continual uproar. There are mobs marching in the street demanding that President Trump step down and allow the great and wonderful Hillary Clinton to be made president by acclamation. Alleged film director Michal Moore is routinely giving the President ultimatums that if he does not step down terrible things will happen. There are those who are given the public trust to work for the protection of this country that are violating that trust by leaking anything and everything that they find out about what our President says, does or even thinks. News outlets are reporting fake news to embarrass the duly elected administration and can't understand why no one trusts them.

Loretta Lynch, the former Attorney General of the United States makes a video where she is talking about fighting and resisting and the fact that there may be blood in the streets. Patrick Stewart, a fine actor, who I greatly respected went on a television show and stated he wanted to become an American citizen so that he can fight! Fight who? About what? Has the fact that Hillary Clinton lost the election, that the American people did not want her, made everyone lose their minds? Grow up, people, elections are for the voters to decide who they want to govern them, we do not have Kings or Queens, nor is Barack Obama the second coming that so many thought he would be.

We have men demanding to go to the women's restrooms, women demanding to go to the men's restrooms and members of Congress are going on tirades about the rights of the transgenders to do these absolutely silly things. I even heard one talking head holding forth on the fact that these desires are protected by the U.S. Constitution. I am sorry, but a careful reading of this document makes no mention of where one might go to relieve oneself.

There are over eleven million illegal (I am sorry, to be politically correct, undocumented immigrants) aliens in this country all screaming over their constitutional rights. A senior member of the California legislature got up in open session to announce that many of his family were here illegally and it violated their constitutional rights to have to hide the fact that they were here illegally[5].

---

[5] Really?

Some of those same members of Congress are making impassioned speeches and marching in the streets demanding that these undocumented immigrants be given full Constitutional rights to include being allowed to vote. One of the headlines in the local newspaper was an immigration attorney stating that an undocumented immigrant has the same rights as a citizen of the United States.

To take this argument further there are tens of thousands of illegals who have been deported for various reasons to include the commission of crimes and then crossed the border again. Members of Congress have even cheered their persistence, not condemned their criminal activity. Mayors of our major cities are stating that they will defy the federal government to protect these law breakers[6].

Even when these people they are protecting commit crimes, to include murder, many of these same mayors and members of Congress go on television, pull their hair and cry real tears screaming that the rights of these law breakers must be protected. Maybe I just imagined it, but I seem to

---

[6] There are 38,428 cases in San Francisco alone, where illegal immigrants are getting their day in court. I, a U.S. citizen and 100% disabled veteran have been denied my day in court for almost 30 years. Is this justice?

remember that those sworn in to public office and charged with enforcing the laws making a promise to "support and defend the constitution".

Many of our elected officials are so concerned trying to protect those from other countries that they forget they were elected to make the lives of their constituents better in this country, not to put them in further jeopardy by helping those from other countries with criminal records to come to this country. I am politically neither a Democrat nor a Republican. I vote for the individual not the party. However, as a former military officer, I was shocked to see our former President more concerned about the rights of the insurgents than those of the American people. He was elected to be the President of the United States not of the world. I even heard one Federal Judge holding forth on how the Constitution is outdated and the wise members of the bench need to make the rules by which we live. Our judges seem to have forgotten that they were appointed or elected to determine and enforce the laws of this country, not give their own opinions to further their own political views.

As another proof that our legal system is not effective, as I was growing up, to publicly threaten to blow up the White House would have gotten the speaker a fast trip to jail courtesy of the Secret Service. Now the speaker, who is a well-known celebrity takes the position that she has a right to threaten the President because she has a first amendment right to say such things under the U.S. Constitution.

A famous rapper, Snoop Dogg has made a rap video showing him assassinating the President and is applauded and another sings about prostituting the First Lady. What has happened to this country? If any of these things had been done in regard to Barack Obama or his wife, there would have been a lynching by the left.

The common denominator among all of these people is that our government and our courts take the position that all of these people have constitutional rights (even those who are here illegally) and the right to due process of law. These so called rights are more important than the rights of the American people not to be victims or to have to live in fear. Attorney's will even offer their services for free[7] to protect these poor immigrants who have broken the law to get here. These immigrants get free legal counsel[8] but I can't represent myself[9] or hire an

---

[7] When has that ever happened before?
[8] Many times at the tax payers' expense.

attorney to represent me who has not been threatened into dropping the case until I found the one I have now.

To even suggest that these people are not entitled to the protection of the U.S. Constitution[10] will bring the wrath of liberalism down on your head. During the first Iraq War I even heard someone argue that if we captured Saddam Hussein he needed to be given his Constitutional Right to a fair trial. I guess the speaker over looked the fact that Saddam was not an American and thus was not entitled to rights under the U.S. Constitution.

As a final straw, when our duly elected president signs an executive order temporarily limiting those from terror sponsoring states from coming here while a vetting program is put in place, everyone, especially Chuck Schumer almost loses their mind screaming about the constitutional rights of those possible terrorists. It must be nice to feel that you are protected by a foreign government and have all of their elected officials falling over themselves to protect those rights you are being given.

---

[9] This is called being pro se and even though it is legal, most judges ignore what a pro se has to say. After all, the pro se is in competition with the members of the Bar.

[10] As members of Congress rant and rave about the Constitutional rights of transgenders, I find it difficult to believe that the founding fathers ever even envisioned such a situation and thus would not and could not have included that in the document upon our government is based.

Though no country in the world, except us, will protect the rights of foreigners over the rights of that country's own citizens.

The government of Mexico is allocating fifty million dollars, some from foreign aid we give them, to protecting the rights of illegals to stay here. Our tax payer dollars are being spent by numerous non-profits to protect the rights of those who have broken the laws of this country by even being here and there are members of Congress who want to give them more taxpayer money to protect more immigrants[11]. Religious institutions are even planning to create an underground railroad to protect those here illegally. Heaven help us!

In fact, it would seem that everyone has constitutional rights and the right to due process, everyone, that is except myself. In the case of an illegal immigrant, the question is were they born here? How did they get here? What does the law say?

In my case, when I try to raise the issue of my Constitution rights, I am told by judges and attorneys alike, why would they say it if it wasn't true? No one bothers to look at the evidence, but rather at who has violated the

---

[11] I am not against immigration, but it needs to be done in a controlled manner rather than throw open the doors and invite everyone in, ala Obama.

most basic premise of our legal system. Is there something wrong with this picture?

CHAPTER TWO
WHO AM I?

It is disheartening to find out that I rank lower than an illegal immigrant in the scheme of things in the country of my birth. The whispers that make the rounds where I live are that I must have committed a terrible crime, though I have never been legally accused of a crime. As a 100% disabled veteran I should have been an easy choice for a job at the local Veteran's Administration, but the State Bar of Georgia raised its head, sent forged documents here and I was denied the job. Of course, when I went for the interview, the first words out of the mouth of the selecting official, a female, non-vet was "*I don't like to work with men.*" Her anti-male bias counted more than my service to this country[12].

Well, perhaps in the minds of some people, I did commit a terrible crime, I represented Black clients against the system in the South. You might ask how so many

---

[12] Had I said that to her, I would have been on the street looking for a job. In her case, she got promoted and spread her anti-male rhetoric even further.

people know about my criminal background, well it seems that some person or persons has made it their mission in life to make sure I am smeared as thoroughly as they can. These baseless allegation show up in the most unusual places.

As an example, a roofing company was hired to replace my roof. Their work was so incompetent that my house was flooded numerous times. They promised to fix everything damaged by their incompetence. However, I discovered they cut a side deal with the insurance company's adjuster for them to be reimbursed by my insurance company for anything they had to spend[13]. I put a stop to it when I found out. The response by the roofing company was to sue me for their reimbursement. During discovery, their attorney took the position that I was at fault because I had stolen money from my clients in Georgia. Their incompetence should be excused because I was a disbarred attorney, never mind the law says that I am not. His attitude is that I am a white male and one of his clients is Hispanic. Ergo, I am at fault.

---

[13] Their attitude, expressed by one of the partners in the roofing company was that why should they have to go to their insurance company and get their rates raised when my company could reimburse them and they would skate with no liability.

So my house, my wife's dream house, is ruined, the roof still leaks (after $38,000.00 for this new roof) our furnishings and mementoes are water damaged, and no one cares. Our homeowner's insurance company, which maintains it "**Stands With You**[14]," has abandoned us, partially based on the fact that I can't be trusted due to what the State Bar of Georgia claimed happened over 25 years ago[15].

The insurance claim has now been open over three years (June of 2014 is when the roof work started) and I can't get the time of day from the Insurance Company or their legal firm in Dallas. I must have really committed a serious crime in Georgia to rate such hatred. I guess I did, I tried to give a Black family an even break.

I was a practicing attorney in Columbus, Georgia. I was not related to anyone in the State Bar[16], I did not go

---

[14] They have blanketed the airwaves with commercials about how they go the extra mile for their clients. In my case, I would agree that they have, in the opposite direction. To show their indifference, there is even a health hazard in the house, toxic mold, that they identified. But they refused to do mold remediation and stopped the main local firm from doing the work. Since I am very allergic to this toxic mold, I guess they are hoping I will die.

[15] One of the owners of the roofing company was heard discussing me and Georgia with the adjuster.

[16] In Georgia at the time, having a relative already practicing counted for a lot.

drinking or carousing with anyone in the State Bar nor was I active in the politics of the State Bar.

I did however, commit a heinous crime in the eyes of the State Bar, I represented a lot of Black clients as well as a lot of Hispanic, Asian and White clients. I did not seek confrontations nor did I run from them. I was a sole practitioner and was content.

Things came to a head when a Black Family[17] came to see me and asked for my help in regard to a bankruptcy case. He was an insurance agent for Nationwide Insurance and worked on a draw. By that I mean that he received a certain amount of money each month and it was expected that he would sell enough insurance each month to pay back the draw. The system works well if you are a go getter and this gentleman was certainly that. His problem was that he had cancer, so he was not his normally hard charging self.

His wife had inherited a full city block of inexpensive rental homes in the direction of the city's expansion. He also owned several building lots in a section of the city known as Green Island Hills, located in the wealthiest part of town.

---

[17] As they were my former clients, I really do not feel I should reveal their names.

As a former Infantry Officer and a 100% disabled veteran, I did not, and do not care what color you are. If you payed me to represent you, that is what I did. I had heard about the pervasive racial discrimination that once marked the town where I practiced, but I had never seen it in action. I was about to get educated.

The family that came to see me wanted to discuss filing bankruptcy and had gone to see another attorney by the name of Fife Whiteside who was well versed in this area of the law. He was an acquaintance and if asked I would have said he was a friend.

I was aware that his mentor was the Bankruptcy Trustee, but really did not put it all together. The Black family had been referred to me by an acquaintance who apparently had assured them that I did not care what the color of their skin was.

During our first meeting I asked them why they preferred to talk to me over Fife M. Whiteside. I told them that I did not do much Bankruptcy work and said that I felt that he would probably do a better job for them. It was at this point that their oldest daughter, who I later found out was a Black Radical who went to the University of Georgia (if memory serves me correctly) spoke up.

She had gone with her parents to see Mr. Whiteside. She told me that after hearing their situation and the assets that they had, Mr. Whiteside had brought in a local building contractor by the name of Cartledge.

Now had Mr. Cartledge and Mr. Whiteside handled matters properly, none of this would have happened and I would probably be in the Georgia Legislature rather than writing this. However, Mr. Cartledge was an older gentleman, a dyed in the wool conservative, a staunch Democrat and a member of the Big Eddy Club[18] as I later discovered. His true feelings came out in what he said to this family[19].

According to the family, during the meeting, Mr. Whiteside had told them that he could arrange things so that they would not have to file bankruptcy and that was why he had brought in Mr. Cartledge. He then turned the meeting over to Mr. Cartledge. According to the daughter, Mr. Cartledge was rather condescending in his approach to the situation and told them that *"people like you don't need*

---

[18] This is a private club made up of the top 425 families in Columbus, Georgia. Here the upper crust met the king makers and made deals affecting us lesser mortals. I was later to learn it was here that my future was decided upon.

[19] He was what was referred to as a yellow dog democrat. By that it is meant that he would rather vote for a yellow dog than a Republican.

to own any property. If you turn it over to me, I will pay off your bills and you can start fresh."

As I remember, this family owed a couple of hundred thousand in debts but their real estate assets literally were worth millions. What Mr. Cartledge was proposing was not a good deal for them, but a fantastic deal for Mr. Cartledge. However, shocked at being talked to in that fashion, their daughter went ballistic and dragged her parents out of the meeting. She felt that Cartledge and Whiteside were trying to take advantage of them.

After hearing the story, I was of two minds about what to do. Clearly, as a sole practitioner, I needed to bring in all of the business that I could, but at the same time, I sensed that this could be a problem if "the fix was in.".

After they left my office, I called Fife Whiteside and told him what they had said. I told him that I really didn't care one way or the other, but it was disturbing because if what they said was true, it smacked of malpractice. I wanted a discussion not start a war.

Instead, Whiteside went crazy. He ranted and raved at me for daring to say such a thing about him. He literally screamed at ne over the phone and ordered me not to represent them and told me that if I did, there would be serious consequences. My response was that I was not going to represent them prior to the phone call, but since he was ordering me not do to so, I would most certainly represent them. Then I hung up[20].

A couple of days later, I was in court representing a client on a minor charge. The Judge in that court was Judge John H. Land. Judge Land was a friend of my father's, they sometimes went bird hunting together, so I knew him fairly well. Of course, I did not know his history, nor his early years that apparently molded him as a man and a judge. As I said earlier, I did not mess with politics much.

When I finished my case, I approached the bench for the Judge to sign an order I had already drawn finding in favor of my client. When he had read and signed the order, he stopped me and invited me to have lunch with him. Though I knew him better than the other judges on the bench, I was still surprised at the invitation. With nothing better to do, I agreed to go to lunch with Judge Land.

Across the street from the court house, an older home had been converted into a very nice restaurant that

---

[20] Later in Bankruptcy court during the first meeting of creditors, the Trustee allowed Whiteside, over my objections since he was not a creditor, to make the case in the record that he had done nothing wrong. He actually allowed Whiteside to cross examine my clients, something that was totally improper. But I was told to shut up and sit down by the Trustee.

basically catered to judges and attorneys. Judge Land had a reserved table and he was treated like royalty.

I later learned that Judge Land was the chief jurist for the Chattahoochee Circuit superior court and was also considered one of the most powerful men in the State of Georgia. He was also the controlling member for a private dining group and a very private freemasonry group known as the **Fish House Gang**[21]. It met originally at a now closed restaurant known as Pritchett's Fish Camp and then later at the Rose Hill Restaurant just to the north of Wynnton. and continues to meet every three or four months for liquor and catfish suppers. The fate of the area and the State of Georgia is often decided over a nice catfish supper by the members of this group.

Had I known about this it would not have meant anything to me, but I later learned that getting an invitation to a catfish supper from John Land was a sign that the

---

[21] In the quarter-century he spent on the bench in the six-county Chattahoochee Judicial Circuit, he was regarded not only as a stern jurist who was tough on crime and on attorneys, but as a behind-the-scenes kingpin who in the political realm could pull strings and yank chains, working through a shadowy association that for meeting in a fish restaurant was known as "The Fish House Gang." Read more here: http://www.ledger-enquirer.com/news/local/article29214088.html#storylink=cpy

behind the scenes leadership[22] of Georgia liked you and a sure sign that you were being groomed for high public office. Well, I blew that as you shall see.

Once we were served our meals, Judge Land opened the conversation by saying that he had watched me work in Court and thought that I had a fine career ahead of me, my only problem was that I didn't not understand a lot of the unwritten rules of the Bar and I didn't know what color I was.

Naturally, I was somewhat taken back and asked him what he meant. He said that I was, and he was sure unknowingly, interfering with some of the perks that other attorneys were entitled to. In fact, he said, some had gone so far as to call me a traitor to my race.

At this point, I was totally baffled. I had no idea what he meant and said so.

"*Son*," he said. "*It is these perks upon which a number of attorney fortunes have been made. By interfering with something being worked on by Mr. Whiteside, you are*

---

[22] Mentioning these unseen rulers might seem like the grossest of conspiracy theory, but they really do control the state of Georgia from behind the scenes and have since the Civil War. I had a friend who was an FBI agent. I told her the story and she took it to her boss. She told me later that he finished the story and named the same names that I did. He said the FBI knew all about these abuses but couldn't make any cases. So they no longer bothered to even investigate.

interfering with a sizable perk to which he is entitled. I have been asked to talk to you and help you see the light.[23]"

I told him that I still had no idea what he was referring to. So he decided to give me some examples.

"Well, let's say that you have a Black client who doesn't have much money, but does own her home. Her son gets into trouble she comes to you to try and get him out of jail. What do you do?"

My response was that I probably could not take the case as she would not have the money to pay a retainer and after all, as much as I would like to help, it was still a business. I also questioned the remark that she probably owned her own home.

"Well, that is where you are missing an opportunity. Many of the Nigras[24] around here own their property

------

[23] I have kept a journal from my military days and tend to write verbatim conversations when it seems advisable to do so. Everyone thought that when I moved from the area and sent all of my papers to storage that I sent the journal as well. Two attorneys showed up at North American Van Lines storage in Florida with a document signed by a Judge saying that I was dead in order to get access to my records. The manager of that facility later tracked me down and told me about what happened.

[24] I am repeating the conversation as close to verbatim as I can. Many older Southerners referred to Blacks as Nigras unless they were in public or on the bench. His referral to "her owning the property" was not in any way to be construed as not being sexist, but it was because

outright as the same family has sometimes lived in the same property for a generation or two. The property may not be worth a lot, but real estate is always a prize if you can get it."

So I asked him to please continue his example and he was very obliging.

"You see, you offer to take a mortgage on her property and let her pay your retainer off so much a month just like a mortgage. If she pays you off, well that's good, however, most of them never had one and probably will not understand what it means. So if you don't explain it to her, she will just keep paying you until she dies. Then you foreclose. You got the money and now you have the property as well."

I considered that for a moment and then asked what if she or her heirs sued over the clear fraud. He laughed and said don't worry about that, if I get on board, not a court in Georgia would rule against me in these matters. I also said that I couldn't see how that applied to me as I had not done anything like that.

His reply was a major surprise.

---

many of the Black families in the area were one parent families with the husband/father either gone or dead.

"Well, there is another way in which attorney's make money and that is through the bankruptcy court. You see, as the attorney you deal one on one with the Trustee. If you see a piece of property you want, and the Trustee has the proper incentive, a straw man can be set up to make a low offer on the property and the Trustee can accept the low offer and then the Straw man sells to you. Neat, simple and clean."

I thought about what he was saying and responded that I did not see how the Bankruptcy Court could be manipulated in the fashion he was suggesting. He smiled and speared another piece of fish.

"Well, it's like this. I will tell you how things really work since I personally think you are merely misguided and once you understand you will see the light.

If a homeowner gets sideways with their financial institution, the financial institution, say a bank, if it wants the property, can impose terms that will force a foreclosure. You know the sad fact is that some people just do not need to own property, they don't know what to do with it. It is the best for everyone that someone who knows how to maximize the value gets the property like in this case.

Once the case is filed with the Bankruptcy Court it falls under the Trustee who in most cases, at least here is not appointed at random but is a standing trustee[25].

Now of course, we have to be fair and make sure everyone gets their fair share of the pie. At this stage there are three professionals appointed under 11 USC Section 327, an attorney, an auctioneer and an appraiser.

Mr. Whiteside is the protégé of the current Trustee, so he is well paid as the attorney. The auctioneer either holds no auction or only those approved by the powers that be are in attendance. Of course, there is the Appraiser, who gets a nice check just signs off on whatever he is told the valuation might be. Until the auction, the property is managed by a property management company that is normally owned by a company owned by the Trustee and the Auctioneer. Once the property is sold at auction to friends, judges, other trustees or some other approved entity it can then be flipped on the open market for a nice return.

---

[25] The Trustee also approves all compensation applications regardless of the requirements of 11 USC, Section 330 which calls for actual and necessary services or expenses. So an unscrupulous insider attorney can demand whatever compensation the traffic will bear and get paid. This is how many Bankruptcy Attorneys make fortunes.

Of course it can also be sold amongst the real insiders for a capital loss or at an inflated price to do a little money laundering."

He paused to take another bite of his lunch and then pointed his fork at me.

"Son, that's what you are interfering with. A member of the Club wants the property that your current Bankruptcy client has and the transaction would have already been concluded except for you getting involved."

I nodded, trying to gel all that he was saying with what I knew about the law. I was being shown an entirely different world of the law and it was a little overwhelming. I asked him what I should do.

He smiled and took another bite.

"Well, son, the best thing would be for you to withdraw as counsel. Everybody will understand that you were just mistaken and really not a race traitor."

I told him that I had already taken their money and filed a notice of appearance with the court. I didn't see how I could get out of it without committing malpractice.

"Just refund their money and I guarantee you that your request to withdraw will be granted with the Court's thanks. You can plead overwork or anything you wish. If a

complaint is filed against you, I guarantee you it will go nowhere."

He continued on before I could say anything.

"*Now I bet you are thinking that everyone will make money out of this deal but you. In the short run that will be true, however, I can assure you that if you desire, you will be admitted to the inner bar of the Bankruptcy Court, become a full-fledged member of the Club.*"

I responded that I had never heard of an inner bar for the Bankruptcy Court. He laughed and waited until his coffee cup had been refilled before he answered.

"*Well, it's not an official bar, you see. It's those attorneys that the Trustee wants to see get ahead. You get first dibs, so to speak, on any property that your client has placed in trust with the Bankruptcy Court and he just might let you quietly bid on other property under his control. Remember, if he decides you get the property, no one can deny you or question his decision, at least not in this court.*"

At that moment, Mr. Cartledge walked in and came over to our table. He looked at me for a moment and then sat down without invitation.

"*You talk any sense into him, yet, Judge?*"

I looked at him for a long moment and then stood. I thanked Judge Land for his invitation and the education, but I was not going to be a part of anything as shady as this was turning out to be. I was going to represent my clients to the best of my ability.

Judge Land looked at me for a long moment and grimaced.

"I respect your courage, young man, but understand that there are many who will consider you a traitor to your race. They will ruin you."

I had no idea how prophetic his words were to be. I week later, a state legislator came to my home to see me. He informed me that he was the leader of the local Klan and that he was going to give me one last chance to get on the right team, God's team, or I would soon not be practicing law.

Looking back, I was probably unwise to do it, but I grabbed him by the collar and the seat of the pants and threw him off my front porch. It was raised off the ground about three feet. I will say that I got some good distance on that toss and he cleared the porch railing by a good foot or so.

CHAPTER THREE
SOME HISTORY OF JUDGE JOHN H. LAND

Before we get much further, I probably ought to make the reader aware of the history regarding Judge John Henry Land that I did not know at the time this all began. I had always thought that he was a fine man and someone to emulate. Boy was I wrong. The old saying about a leopard not being able to change his spots is very definitely true, especially in the case of Judge Land.

During the few times that the State Bar would condescend to talk to me about these matters, they always asked why I thought Judge Land would turn against me. I never had an answer and he would not talk to me. It was only recently that I discovered why Judge Land would consider me a traitor to the white race.

Judge John Henry Land was one of ten children born into a large and very powerful Georgia family. Georgia in the early 20th century was very much as it had been during and after the civil war. White's ruled, by that I mean wealthy whites and Blacks (and non-wealthy whites) walked softly and kowtowed to the Masters. If a Black killed a white, there had to be swift justice that normally resulted in the death penalty. If a White killed a Black there was often no punishment at all. In 1912, this was especially true.

The trying of serious crimes for much of Georgia below Atlanta, especially the counties which were encompassed by the Chattahoochee Circuit, which included Harris County, was handled in the Superior Court of Columbus. In 1912 and for many years after that Sterling Price Gilbert[26] was the superior Court Judge. He was later to be a Georgia Supreme Court jurist.

During this time period, there were a number of instances where mobs took prisoners from the jail and hung them in the woods outside of Columbus, there was little in the way of punishment for these criminals. While you may wonder why I digress, you will shortly see why this is important to what happened.

On June 30, 1912, Cedron "Cleo" Land, the cousin of the not yet born John H. Land, was sent to the field in order to pasture a mule. The family farm, located in the county and some said extended over into Harris County was rather extensive. So when he failed to return by

---

[26] Named after Confederate General Sterling Price.

nightfall, his family was concerned, but not unduly. Several members set out to look for him.

According to the Columbus Ledger[27], it was around 2:00 AM when Cleo's body was found in an out of the way place with a wound in his left eye. An examination showed that he had taken a shotgun blast in the face, and almost the whole load of shot had lodged in his brain. It was believed that he had died instantly. Tracks found near the body led to the home of T.Z. "Teasy" McElhaney.

Though the two boys were of different races and such associations were certainly frowned on in polite company, Teasy, as he was called was known to be a playmate of Cleo. John Beahn, a Columbus Bailiff confronted Teasy and eventually got a confession out of him[28]. I might point out that the methods in which confessions are elicited today are drastically different from how it was done in 1912.

Beahn based arresting the boy primarily on a shotgun he found at the boy's home and some bloody clothes and sacks that had been hidden[29]. Bean presumed

---

[27] The local newspaper.

[28] Rose, David, The Big Eddy Club: The Stocking Stranglings and Southern Justice, The New Press, New York.

[29] After all, Teasy had a shotgun in his home, Cleo was killed by a shotgun, therefore, Teasy was guilty. However, owning a shotgun in the rural south in 1912 was not an unusual event, unless you are Black

the boy had hidden the items to cover up his commission of the crime. He later testified that on the way to jail, the boy admitted that he was with Cleo Land when the was killed, but claimed that it was an accident. Most of the evidence submitted to the court was based on Beahn's unsupported words[30].

Cleo was buried beside his late mother, Lula Land at the Mount Moriah Primitive Baptist Church later that same day, so much for gathering evidence from the body. The family claimed that it was a hot summer and they could not afford to wait before burying their son. Hundreds of the Land family and friends came for the impromptu funeral.

During the gathering, there were rumors that the negro would be taken and lynched if he was brought to the courthouse for a hearing. The County Sheriff, Jesse Beard, deputized seven extra men to guard the jail. They would be a lot of good against a mob of hundreds of their friends and neighbors.

Judge W.H. McCrory, a junior colleague of Judge Price Gilbert, was assigned to deal with Teasy's pretrial hearing on July 5th. Afraid that the prisoner would be

---

and the dead boy is the son of a very wealthy White family. Instant promotion for Beahn eventual death for the Black accused.

[30] Beahn's own testimony as reported in the Ledger.

murdered if he was taken to the courthouse, he decided to convene his court at the jail. There he heard a summary of Teasy's all-too plausible account of what had happened. Cleo and he had been projecting[31] with the gun, and the gun went off and killed Cleo. The defendant said he came back home, tried to wash up the blood and didn't tell anyone it was accident because he was afraid. Judge McCrory sat the boy's trial was fixed for August.

A superior court grand jury empaneled by Judge Sterling Price Gilbert indicted Teasy McElhaney for murder on August 5. The makeup of that superior court grand jury is interesting to note. Its members included Cleo Land's uncles R.E.L. (Ed") Land and Aaron Brewster Land[32]. Of course no one in Columbus found this a

---

[31] Slang for playing with the gun, pretending to shoot at targets or each other. Neither had apparently checked to see if the gun was loaded. It was.

[32] Aaron Brewster Land helped murder Simon Adams, a 19-year old Black farm laborer who was caught trying to burgle the house of Judge E.H. Almond, in 1900. When apprehended, Adams was trying to hide in the bedroom of Almond's two daughters, so the assumption was he had come to rape the white girls. Aaron Brewster Land was the bailiff assigned to escort Adams to Columbus for incarceration in the country jail. Instead of taking the direct route to Columbus, Land took another road that ended in a dead-end. Waiting for Land and his prisoner were masked vigilantes who took Adams and drug him to Lover's Leap where they pushed him into the river. He was bound with a chain around his neck. When he was too long in drowning, one of the vigilantes used his rifle to shoot Adams. However, wisely, he ducked under the surface, coming up only to gasp for a breath of air. Finally,

conflict of interest and no one asked the defendant or even cared what his opinion might be about close relatives of the dead boy sitting on the Grand Jury. The true bill having been returned[33], trial was scheduled for August 13, 1912.

Judge Gilbert appointed three lawyers to represent young McElhaney at the trial. Jurys are normally to be formed from the peers of the accused. Both Cleo Land and Teasy McElhaney were the sons of farmers. However, no one on the jury was a farmer, but were rather the jurors were drawn from the ranks of the city's more prosperous members of the white community. They included engineers, four businessmen, two salesmen, a bookkeeper and a tailor[34]. McElhaney's parents also had no involvment at all in the trial.

At the trial, the main testimony against the defendant came from Will Land, the father of Cleo Land, the victim. Of course, he had not been present when his son was killed but a little thing like that was not going to help the defendant.

---

one of the bullets hit him in the back of the head as he came up for air. In spite of losing his prisoner under suspicious circumstances, Land was still appointed as a Deputy Sheriff in 1905, which showed that losing a Black prisoner to vigilantes was not considered a very serious incident.

[33] What a shock!

[34] Rose, David, The Big Eddy Club: The Stocking Stranglings and Southern Justice, The New Press, New York.:

There was little question that Teasy may have had something to do with Cleo's death, but the evidence that it was anything other than an accident was very weak. When asked, the defendant, barefoot, wearing a pair of shorts and a short sleeved shirt at his trial said: "*I am just a little black nigger and I knew if I went to Mr. Land and told him that I had killed his boy, he would kill me. I was afraid to tell him so I hid the body.*"

A Georgia Courtroom in the summertime, especially in 1912 with only a few ceiling fans trying to move the hot air, can get as hot as the hinges of hell many of the participants should go to. So it was not surprising that the jury deliberations only took a short time. After all, the jurors being business men had their businesses to get back to and they could not be bothered to waste a lot of time on this foolishness.

At 5:00 PM the same day as the trial had begun, the jury foreman read the verdict. The jury had found the defendant guilty of manslaughter in the commission of an unlawful act, not murder as the prosecutor's office had demanded[35]. Judge Gilbert handed down the harshest sentence the law allowed, three-years hard labor at the penitentiary. Though being Black and being sent to the

---

[35] Manslaughter is a lesser included offense to the charge of murder.

penitentiary for killing a White was probably a death sentence in and of itself, it was not what the public wanted and certainly not what the Land family wanted.

Having concluded business for the day, Judge Gilbert, the lawyers and the women in the public gallery got up and left the court. It was later commented on the fact that they all seemed to leave the courtroom in some haste, but maybe they were just going someplace to try and get cooler[36].

What happened next was reported in the Enquirer-Sun newspaper.

THE MURDER OF T. Z. MCELHANEY

According to the Enquirer-Sun, trouble began when two unarmed bailiffs[37], R.L. Willis and J. T. Darby, were moving the defendant from the courtroom to the sheriff's office. Gathered in the aisles of the courtroom, blocking the path were numerous friends and relatives of the dead boy. It was estimated that this group numbered twenty-five or

---

[36] Weeks before the trial Cleo's father had gone to see Sheriff Beard and warned him if the verdict was anything less than murder, that there would be trouble.

[37] Though there had been threats of violence against the defendant, the bailiffs were unarmed. This should speak loud and clear about whether or not the kidnapping was known by the Sheriff and the Court officials. Couldn't have the bailiffs wound or kill any fine upstanding members of the White community while protecting a Black prisoner, now could we?

so. Before the bailiffs could leave the courtroom, the door was blocked and the twenty-five or so men in the courtroom surrounded the defendant and his escorts. They demanded that the prisoner be turned over to them. The two bailiffs maintained later that they refused to surrender their prisoner.

At this point, it was reported that one of the vigilantes struck Bailiff R.L. Willis in the face. Another was said to have dealt him a heavy blow. Under attack, he understandably released his prisoner to defend himself. What was reported as a strenuous fisticuff followed.

Then according to Bailiff Darby the prisoner was torn away from Darby and a big man hurled the officer several feet into the courthouse rotunda, the fight having left the courtroom and moved into the rotunda. Hearing the noise, Deputy Sheriff Gibson came running to help and was disabled by being kicked in the stomach.

As the strenuous fisticuffs raged, the group that now had control of Teasy was moving him toward the front door of the courthouse. Aware that he probably did not have long to live if they got him outside the court house, Teasy was screaming for help, but no one came to his rescue and apparently business as usual continued around the fighters.

As the first group struggled to get Teasy outside, a second band of armed men blocked the courthouse door to keep Sheriff Beard and his deputies from following[38].

From the evidence it was clear that this mob did not want to kill Teasy inside the city limits. But if they would get him to the wilds of the county, well then the Columbus police could not (or better said would not) follow them.

Now they were faced with getting away with their prisoner. In 1912, there were not a lot of cars in Columbus, there were horses, mules or maybe farm wagons or buggies, but not a lot of fast cars that could carry 20 or 25 men and a struggling prisoner. So what did these fighters for truth justice and American Way do? Well, surprisingly enough at that moment a street car, Number 18, came along on the east side of 10th Street. Just as it reached the west side of 2nd Avenue, a pistol was pointed at the motorman who immediately stopped the car[39].

There were said to be passengers already on the car who immediately got off. According to the story, one

---

[38] Too bad that this courthouse only had one exit, the front door. If only there were other doors leading outside or maybe some windows that had opened to the outside, enterprising deputies could have gotten outside and behind the group blocking the front door. "*For want of a nail, the shoe was lost.*

[39] Try finding a cap or a street car exactly when you need one. This was clearly a miracle. God must have been on the side of the vigilantes.

vigilante held a pistol on the motorman and another on the conductor. The street car took them to the city limits and dropped off the vigilantes and their prisoner[40].

Interestingly enough, one of the reasons given later for the law officers not giving chase was that no one knew which way the kidnappers had gone. However, though they escaped on a streetcar, no one thought to follow the tracks. Once they left the streetcar, there a stretch of woods and just beyond that the armed vigilantes filled Teasy McElhaney full of lead as the expression goes.

Now even though there were claims no one knew which way the kidnappers had gone once they left the Courthouse, other witnesses reported that by the time the vigilantes and their prisoner had gone but a few blocks on 10th Street the street was alive with excited people who were following the streetcar and who wanted to see what happened next.

Automobiles, motorcycles, buggies and other forms of transportation filled the street, with many other people following on foot. Apparently everyone in town, except the sheriff and his deputies knew there was going to be a killing and they wanted to watch.

---

[40] Surprisingly in this otherwise complete recitation of what the vigilantes did, there is not one mention of any attempt to give chase on the part of the Sheriff or his deputies. Must have been an over sight.

The Muscogee county coroner, J.S. Tefty and his six-man coroner's jury went to the scene of the shooting, examined the body and held an immediate inquest on the spot. It was reported that the Coroner said it was impossible to tell how many bullets had been fired into the body. It was later estimated that there were between 25 and 50 bullet holes found in the dead boy's body.

No one who was found at the scene of the crime would later state whether they knew any of the men engaged in the killing, or at least, they refused to state names. It was possible to say how many men had been on the streetcar with their prisoner, because these desperate killers had actually bought 18 tickets for themselves and one for their prisoner from the conductor, who had said he was in fear of his life, but no so fearful he could not sell tickets. Clearly these heavily armed kidnappers bought tickets because they did not want to break the law.

As expected, the coroner's verdict was that Teasy met his death at the hands of persons unknown.

Before this incident, no white person had ever stood trial for murdering a Black in Columbus, Georgia. However, Judge Gilbert was outraged at what had happened, or so he said. I am sure that Teasy was comforted that some of the more prominent women in the city's charitable clubs and several ministers circulated petitions condemning the execution.

Judge Gilbert went in front of the Muscogee County Grand Jury and made a very impressionable speech (he was up for reelection after all and Blacks could vote) asking for an indictment in regard to the death. A preliminary investigation had revealed that the abduction of Teasy McElhaney was led by none other than Cleo Land's father, Will Land and his brothers Ed and Brewster Land. The first major obstacle to the issuance of these indictments was that Ed and Brewster Land both sat on the Muscogee County Grand Jury. They were actually asked to vote on their own indictments.

Judge Gilbert managed to light a fire under the Grand Jury as they came back with three indictments and later added a fourth. Those charged were Ed and Brewster Land and a millworker by the name of Lee Lynn. They were charged with the murder. A later indictment added the name of Will Land, though he was charged only with unlawfully using a firearm[41], hardly a charge to warrant a grand jury indictment, but it was issued anyway.

---

[41] I would have to guess that the shooting of a screaming prisoner would fall under unlawful discharging of a firearm.

Now you would think that Sheriff Beard and his deputies would be eager to go out and bring in the culprits who had been responsible for humiliating them in the courthouse. Not so, as the Land Brothers mysteriously vanished for 3 months, not that the sheriff or his men made much of effort to find them.

The wanted fugitives did not reappear until they drove up to the courthouse in Columbus on November 5th. It seems no one noticed them driving from their homes to the courthouse. Brewster Land spoke for the three when he said: *"We have not been running away from justice. The only thing was that we did not wish to lie in jail until the next term of court."* Interesting thing is that I cannot find another murder suspect who was offered this choice. Such was the power of the Land family.

The prosecution had also made a serious error. The solicitor that was to handle the prosecution was George Palmer. He had charged them with murder, with no lesser included offenses included in the charge. As he began to put his witnesses on the stand a peculiar thing began to emerge. Everyone, to include the Sheriff and his Deputies demonstrated amnesia as to certain facts.

Though numerous people witnessed the shooting at the execution site the sheriff and his deputies could not find, no one could remember who was doing the shooting. None of the deputies that had been beaten at the courthouse could remember who did the beating. They could remember that Brewster Land was present helping block the courthouse door, but he wasn't charged with that, only with murder.

The prosecution had to prove who did the shooting, which it could not and that the Land Brothers were involved in a conspiracy to kill Teasy McElhaney, which was tough since none of the witnesses could place the defendants at the scene of the killing.

Several other passengers on the streetcar heard Teasy McElhaney begging his captors not to kill him, but for some reason they could not remember who he had been directing his pleas to. It was just the strangest thing, but no one could remember anything that put the Lands at the scene of the murder.

On the second day of this unusual murder trial, the first trial in the State of Georgia where Whites were on trial for the murder of a Black, the jury went into deliberations at 11:00 AM and were back by 11:29 AM. The foreman of the jury S.W. Dudley read the verdict in a loud and clear voice. "*Not Guilty*!"

Later it was discovered that the verdict had been arrived at with no discussion as soon as they had walked into the jury room. The case was over, the three accused, that everyone was pretty sure had organized and carried out the murder of this Black teenager, were free. There was not even a mention made of their escape from the law, after all, I guess it was clear to everybody that sitting in jail until the next court session would be somewhat inconvenient to these powerful landowners.

This is the family that gave birth to and raised John Henry Land from boy to man. He was raised as an ardent segregationist as he admitted in numerous interviews in his later years though he claimed he had evolved to a new understanding about race[42]. However, based upon his treatment of me due to my representation of Blacks, he never changed his beliefs.

---

[42] http://www.ledger-enquirer.com/news/local/article29214088.html

WHY WOULD THEY SAY IT   /53

CHAPTER FOUR
<u>THEY</u> WANT YOU TO RESIGN

It was shortly after that fateful lunch with Judge Land when the campaign to get rid of me began. I received a call from Paul B. Cohen[43] an assistant General Counsel with the State Bar of Georgia. He wasted no time in informing me that I was required to resign as an attorney. I asked him why I was supposed to resign and his only response was that *"they wanted me to!"* I asked who they were and he refused to tell me, but just kept repeating they want you to resign I naturally refused.

I asked Mr. Cohen what I had done that required my resignation. His response was that it did not matter, as they wanted me to resign. He assured me that if I resigned, I would be shortly invited to be a member again. I asked if I had done something serious enough to require that I resigned, where were the charges, when was the hearing supposed to be and when was I to be served with service of

---

[43] Now a prominent attorney in Atlanta.

process. He laughed and said that I just did not get it. I was to resign and none of that other stuff mattered. I responded with a firm no. So began the campaign to destroy my practice.

No relatively new sole practitioner can hope to survive in a law practice without having a good relationship with a bank. I had my accounts with Columbus Bank and Trust (CB&T) and had maintained accounts with them since I was 18.

Almost before I hung up from that telephone call, my credit line with that bank was closed. My ability to take credit cards from my clients for payment of their fees which was arranged through that bank was terminated. Even my credit card issued through that bank which I had maintained since I was a Second Lieutenant in the Army was closed[44]. I asked my banker what was going on and why this was happening and was told that it was just business. He refused to discuss it further.

Other attorneys with whom I had maintained friendly relations for several years suddenly wanted to have

---

[44] In those days when you were commissioned as an officer, as part of the in-processing to your first duty station, you went by a station where you were issued a credit card. The idea was that in those days all officers were required to be members of the Officers' Club, rather you used it or not, and your dues were charged to that credit card.

nothing to do with me. One even went so far as to tell my secretary, Beverly Suhr, to tell me that I should watch my back, but refused to speak to me about what he meant[45].

Even my account with a business supply store where I had spent a great deal of money, was closed and the owner sent people to repossess my office furniture, even though it was almost entirely paid for. When I asked the owners of the business supply company why they were acting this way, I was told it was just business and their attorneys had told them not to discuss it with me.

I asked if I was late on payments or owned them anything I had not paid and was assured that my payment record with them was excellent, but they could not tell me why they were doing these things.

My secretary suddenly wanted to have nothing to do with me and quit. She finally told me that her friends in the courthouse told her that she had to get away from me as I

---

[45] I later learned that I was being followed. It eventually got so bad that I reported it to the police who just laughed at me. It seemed that they knew who was following me. It turned out that Judge Land wanted to know who I was associating with. I guess when you are considered a traitor to your race, you have to be watched. Such was my mental state in those days with everything falling apart that when they got too insistent on following me, I stepped into the street with my pistol in my hand and dared them to continue. The two off duty police officers assigned to follow me left me alone after that, or at least kept their distance.

had stolen over $500,000.00 from my clients[46]. I confronted the people (other attorneys and their secretaries) she told me had spread this rumor and they said that the story had come from the State Bar so it had to be true. Evidence be damned.

Finally, I had no choice but to close my office. I was under pressure from my then wife to continue her one-. woman campaign to treat her daughter (my step-daughter) like a princess. Her daughter had Wortnig-Hoffman Neurological Syndrome which left her in a wheelchair. Such was her daughter's view of the world that she insisted that she be given everything she wanted when she wanted it. I felt that she and brother should be treated equally, but that did not meet with her approval and she was able to twist her mother around her finger by insinuating that it was her mother's fault that she, the daughter, was in the wheelchair.

So her mother, my wife, hammered at me to give the girl everything she wanted. It also seems that the daughter who did not like me, was being fed the stories about my alleged criminal activity from her friends who

---

[46] Every client that I ever had, their families and their dogs did not have $500,000.00 between them. When I asked where the proof was for these charges, I was told *"Why would they say it if it wasn't true?"* That seemed to satisfy most people, even judges and attorneys who had been friends.

were getting it from their parents, who were getting it from the legal community. So much for innocent until proven guilty.

Just as things were looking very dim, a friend of mine, Charles R. Davis, introduced me to a friend of his, Laurence Lyman, an attorney from Florida. We had worked together in regard to a case involving Mr. Davis so we knew each other fairly well. At the urging of Mr. Davis, Mr. Lyman offered me a position with his firm in Pinellas County, Florida and I gladly accepted.

I sold my practice to Peter C. Quezada, a former deputy sheriff who had become an attorney. The day he came to pick up the files, Charles R. Davis was in my office and witnessed the transaction. Part of the deal was that Mr. Quezada would step into my shoes and then get the attorney's fees due on the various cases from settlements that were pending.

The receipt for the files signed by Mr. Quezada was placed in a file regarding the closing of my practice along with copies of the informational letters sent out to each client as required by the State Bar rules[47].

---

[47] As soon as I left the area, Mr. Quezada called each of my former clients into his office and demanded large retainers, which was not part of the agreement. When they objected, he took the files back to my empty office which was opened by the building management for him

In late 1987, I moved my family down to Treasure Island, Florida[48]. I reported to Mr. Lyman's Office in St. Petersburg, Florida to begin work and start preparing for the Florida Bar Exam. For a few weeks everything was fine, but then one day he called me into his office, told me this could not work out as he was being harassed by Mr. Cohen and threatened with sanctions for hiring a crook.

One day I received a call from an investigator for the State Bar of Georgia by the name of Ed Shay. He was the one who told me that Quezada had abandoned my clients and dumped their files on the floor in my empty office. I asked Mr. Shay if I should return to Georgia and take over those cases again and he said not to bother as it was no big deal. It happens all of the time.

A few days later, according to Mr. Lyman, he received a called from Paul B. Cohen that the State Bar of Georgia was going to file a formal complaint against him with the Florida Bar for hiring me. I protested that I had not

---

and he dumped the files the middle of the floor. I was not informed. He was later exonerated of any wrongdoing by the Office of the General Counsel of the State Bar of Georgia, the same entity that employed Mr. Paul B. Cohen.

[48] The step-daughter, who was 18 insisted that she be left in Columbus, Georgia in a nice apartment. She did not want anything to do with me, except for my money of course. She along with the other problems I was facing, I was required to send my wife by air to check on her daughter every few weeks.

been charged or even accused of any wrongdoing, but he said those words that I would come to hate – *WHY WOULD THEY SAY IT IF IT WASN'T TRUE*? My Florida legal career was over before it really began so I returned to Columbus, Georgia.

My then wife had the unique ability to antagonize people who should have been friends. In her mind, no one was good enough for her and her precious daughter. Unfortunately, I literally had nothing in my pocket when I arrived back in Columbus, Georgia. Charles Davis offered me a place to stay but was very clear that neither he nor his wife could stand my wife and did not want her around. Finally, another friend that I had helped when in practice, John C. Touchton offered to take us in temporarily. He lived in Waverly Hall, Georgia a small community just outside of Columbus. I gratefully accepted.

Eventually, since I still had a license to practice law in Georgia, I returned to Waverly Hall, Georgia and opened a practice in the little community and began to build up another client base. Apparently, I was still being watched since Paul B. Cohen started calling the Touchton home demanding that I resign my license to practice law.

Though I had been in contact with Ed Shay of the State Bar several times, Paul B. Cohen notified me that there were several pending complaints against me and he planned to file an action that I was hiding to avoid answering the numerous complaints against me. I asked him to send the complaint to me and he said that there were 14 but he would send the worst five. I responded to those five and they were dismissed.

The next time that Paul B. Cohen contacted me he informed me that this was getting us nowhere and I need to resign. Again I said no. He then referred me to a special master by the name of Timothy Adams. Adams said any resignation would be no big deal and I would be readily readmitted should I want to return to Georgia.

Finally, I submitted a letter that said simply "I quit." Paul Cohen called in response and said he would only accept a resignation that was drafted to his specifications.

My then wife had apparently been contacted by the State Bar of Georgia and told I was a bad person and that she had to get away from me. I had bought a small house out in the country and she accepted an invitation from a neighbor for us to come to dinner. While we were eating, she excused herself to go to the bathroom, met her son outside and they walked down to the road and were picked up by one of her friends from work and they disappeared. So much for her standing by her man. I was left looking like an idiot, but that seemed to be par for the course with her and her children[49].

The last straw for me in Georgia was when Paul B. Cohen threatened to bring an action against me for abandoning my clients. I pointed out that I had not abandoned anyone, that I had notified them and even sent them letters as required when one closed a practice. He responded that I would need the client records to prove I had sent them letters and that they had all been returned to them clients. I responded that I would simply contact them and he laughed at me. He informed me that if I called even one of them that he would charge me with harassment. Any attempts to prove that I had not done anything wrong would be met with a court order stopping me from proving I had done nothing wrong. Again he insisted that I resign.

I was starting to get back on my feet when I received an envelope in my office in Waverly Hall. Inside the envelope was a picture of my wife with a bullseye on her face and threats to harm John Touchton's young son

---

[49] Later I was made aware that her son would not return to live under my roof unless I took some of the money that I had stolen from my clients and set him up a $100,000.00 trust fund. As it was, in an attempt to embarrass me, he checked into a hotel for abandoned and abused children with over $15,000.00 in musical instruments that I had given him. I was never sure what the definition of abandoned and abused was in regard to him.

Andrew. The message was clear. Leave or they die. That was it for me.

As for the marriage, it was broken beyond repair as far as I concerned. She had told me that she really didn't care about me, that I was just a paycheck for her to take care of her children, both of whom hated me at this point, the daughter because I would not shower her with money and treat her like the queen she thought she was and the son because he was told do to so by his mother.

As for Andrew, he was a special needs child and was a sweet as he could be. I could not place him in jeopardy by staying and trying to make a fight of it. After long and hard thought I accepted an offer to join a company in California.

In 1990, I applied to take the Bar Exam in California. The General Counsel, Margaret Warren called me and informed me that even if I passed the Bar that I would not be admitted. She said that Paul B. Cohen of the Georgia Bar had called her and told her than I was disbarred (not true) and that I had stolen huge sums of money from my clients (also not true). I told her that I had not been disbarred and that if there was a charge against me, I was not aware of it. Her response was to say why would he say if it wasn't true. California did not want an issue with Georgia.

I took the Bar, passed and was denied entrance even though the Bar rules at that time said that I had the right to a hearing to prove I had not received due process in Georgia. She denied me even the opportunity for that hearing to prove that I was correct as she said Cohen threatened to sue the California Bar to stop my admission. *I Never really had a chance.*

After hearing a speech by Nancy Pelosi where she talked about the rights of the people, I called her office asking for help, pointing out my most basic rights were taken from me. I could not even get an appointment. Today, she is a staunch supporter that the world apparently has the right to due process, but apparently not a white male, veteran.

CHAPTER FIVE
A NEW CAREER

Well, it was something of a shock to find out that such was the power of the State Bar of Georgia that they could bar me from practicing in other states with a mere phone call. They did not have to prove that I done anything wrong, just make unsupported allegations and back them up with the power of the State Bar. Truth and justice meant nothing to anyone, since the new form of evidence consisted of *"Why Would They Say It If It Wasn't True!"*[50]

However, it is California who was, and is, busting a gut to protect the rights of immigrants over the rights of natural born American citizens. However, in my case, no

---

[50] I find it interesting that the same state that is willing to go bankrupt to support and defendant illegal immigrants was not willing to give an American citizen and a veteran the opportunity for a hearing. Could it be that there is a working relationship between state bars that goes far beyond what is wise and just? Could we be looking at a conspiracy to violate civil rights?

one wanted to see the evidence that my rights had been violated. I guess this is the mind-set of the liberal left that has always controlled California. White males need not apply, all others welcome, here legally or not.

I am not talking political philosophies here, but rather the hard and unfair way things are done in the great state of California. I watched incompetent buffoons lauded as brilliant attorneys and I could not even get a job as a para-legal because Georgia was stalking me to ensure that I could not succeed. What is even worse is that no one wanted to hear it when I talked of being denied my civil rights, but there was plenty of time and money to help those who had broken the laws to be here, evade the laws of the land.

So I looked for something I could do to earn a decent living. It was hard to go from making a six figure income to not having a dime in my pocket. I had helped a lot of people as an attorney, but no one wanted to help me. Then I discovered insurance and fell into an estate planning position. I took the test for an insurance license and then obtained an investment license to sell mutual funds and then found a company with an opening where I could learn the business. Once again, allowed to use my abilities, I began to establish an income stream.

I worked hard and began to make a name for myself in sales. Soon I was noticed by the big companies and was hired by Metropolitan Life (MetLife) to sell life insurance and mutual funds. I was assigned to the office in Orange County. My manager was Dominic Sanfelippo. He taught me a lot about how to sell and deal with people. He also taught me how to create an unfair advantage and stab a fellow worker in the back. However, first the good part.

My first year, my sales were good enough that I was invited to the sales convention in La Jolla, CA for the top sales people. It was there that I met my current wife. She was also a top sales person in her office. We just hit off.

While at the initial cocktail party for attendees, Dominic said that he was concerned that I might leave the firm. He went on to say that I needed a wife that understood the business. He told me to look around the room and pick out a female, any female and he would set me up.

Across the room was the executive vice president's daughter, an attractive blonde who's name I don't remember. She was talking to a very pretty dark haired girl. I pointed to the executive vice-president's daughter and said if you are serious I want her.

His response was to say, well I don't recommend her, she's pushy and can be a handful, but if you are serious I'll be right back. After a few moments, he returned with the EVP's daughter and the pretty girl she had been talking to. It didn't really work out with the EVP's daughter, but I eventually married the pretty girl she had been talking to.

The young lady and I enjoyed each other's company. The only problem was that she was based in New Mexico and I was based in California. This seemed to be an insurmountable problem until her boss offered me a position in his office. In short order I had moved to New Mexico and started to work building a new client base. I began to notice that a number of my clients in California were dropping the policies and then re-writing them with the same MetLife office.

I discovered that Dominic Sanfelippo was approaching my clients, getting them to drop the policies that they had with me and then re-writing them under his name. This is called churning and is illegal unless you are good friends with the senior management at MetLife, then it is fine. At the time, they were mostly Italian and I was not – what a lesson I was learning about how to be discriminatory.

I had been in New Mexico about six months when I was asked to make a presentation about the use of trusts to a businessman's group. Though I was not allowed to practice law, I had worked with trusts for a period and was familiar with how insurance trusts worked.

One afternoon, I received a call from a man who began the conversation with "Are you happy?" I thought it was a religious call. It was not, it was a call from a recruiter for Merrill, Lynch. He had heard my presentation and wanted to offer me a job to write insurance for Merrill, Lynch customers. He invited me to fly to New Jersey to their training campus for a talk. I leveled with the man and told him about the Georgia Bar and the fact that I was engaged to someone in New Mexico.

He said don't worry about the Georgia situation, just don't bring it up unless directly asked by a superior and as for my fiancé, that was easily solved. They offered her a job as well. She was assigned to be my assistant. It says a lot about her that she took the position. In some areas she knew more about insurance than I did.

After my training session, I was told they were going to send me someplace warm – it turned out to be New York City. I was to write policies for the clients of the

Merrill Lynch office located in the Pan Am Building which is attached to Grand Central Station. What a change.

We were required to pay for our own move and make all of the arrangements ourselves. So we paid movers to pack a U-Haul and left Albuquerque, New Mexico and drove to New York City. We had found an apartment on East 77th Street and were very happy. Work was going great, I was writing bigger and bigger policies for Merrill Lynch clients and all seemed right with the world.

The interesting thing about my wife is that she has never met a stranger. She can go into a room where she knows no one and in thirty minutes, be on a first name basis with half the room. Well one afternoon, she was crossing the street and had a conversation with the person walking beside her. He was from the Philippines and had just been appointed to be the Ambassador to the Court of St. James (England). He had no idea what to do with the apartment he owned in New York City. This apartment was in Trump Tower. By the time they had reached the other side of the street, she had sublet the apartment. She came home and told me that we were moving to Trump Tower at 56th and 5th.

Once again we had to handle the move ourselves at our own expense. We rented a truck and packed it ourselves. We also had a car in the city so I drove a lot of things over in the car. The building had a freight elevator that was large enough to handle a car and so I drove to the basement loading dock and carried everything up to the apartment (35C). There were also some parking spaces and storage units, but I was told they had all been earmarked by Ivana. It was a one-bedroom apartment, but it was great.

The first time I entered the lobby to get the Concierge to allow me to drive into the elevator, Donald Trump and Ivana were in the lobby, Ivanka and her brother were doing the can-can on the Concierge desk. I introduced myself to Mr. Trump[51] and went on about my business[52].

I was enjoying the work I was doing and found out that I was good at it. Unfortunately, I also found out that there were those who were not so happy with my job performance. I was being too successful in their eyes.

One day I was informed by a representative of Merrill Lynch's oversight department that a complaint had been filed against me. I asked which of my clients had a

---

[51] Now of course, President Trump.

[52] I discovered later that Mr. Trump does not miss much and has a very good memory. A few days later I ran into him in the lobby and he called me by name. Very impressive. I am also thoroughly familiar with the layout of the building and the young lady who accused Mr. Trump of coming on to her in the building clearly has never been beyond the Concierge Desk. He was rarely alone during the almost three years we lived there and always the consummate gentleman.

problem so that I could address it. I was then told that it was a couple named Sayatovic[53] from Beverly Hills, California that I had known while working for MetLife.

Merrill Lynch treated this complaint as a complaint about wrong doing. I was called on the carpet, accused of wrongdoing and not allowed to really defend myself. That is until my wife who was called to testify against me at the internal hearing asked why someone who was not even a MetLife policy holder was allowed to make such a silly complaint[54].

At this point I asked the hearing officer to clarify what the charges against me were. The hearing officer turned red, stuttered, went through his papers a dozen times, ignored me and asked her if she was sure that they were not a policy holder. She confirmed they were not ever a policy holder. He closed his folder, got to his feet and said this hearing was over and walked out. No apology to

---

[53] I think his first name was Mark Sayatovic, he was drawing disability from a radio station. Interestingly enough their complaint was not that I had done something wrong but that I would not return to California and represent him in front of the IRS. While practicing I had done some of that, but he was well aware that I was not a California attorney and could not represent him.

[54] The complaint was that I would not return to California to help with his IRS problem. Though I had stressed I was not an attorney, he kept insisting that I could talk for him at the IRS since he was disabled. So he thought if he complained to Merrill Lynch, they would make come represent him.

me for the baseless allegations, and forcing me to go through a baseless hearing.

I thought the matter was over, but I was not aware that the internal review department of Merrill Lynch had a reputation of never losing once they accused an employee of wrongdoing. Being cleared of charges was not in the vocabulary of this department. Though I had been cleared of any wrongdoing, Robert Brain Sensale, an attorney for the internal review department decided that I had to be guilty of something, he just had to find it.

Somehow he got in touch with the State Bar of Georgia and Paul B. Cohen and was told I had stolen money from my clients and been disbarred. He didn't ask for proof of any wrongdoing on my part, he just took Cohen's unsupported word. In Georgia, and at Merrill Lynch, accusations equal guilt.

I was called in front of the EVP for New York City and told that I was fired immediately for being disbarred and not tell anyone. I asked if I was not entitled to prove this was not true and was told by Mr. Sensale that they knew all they need to know, after all, why would Georgia say it if it wasn't true. I returned to my office in the Pan Am Building and I was immediately thrown out of the building on orders of Mr. Sensale. When my wife came home she told me she had been called in and told that she exercised poor judgement by marrying a crook[55] and she was fired as well. I guess this was true guilt by association. Such is due process as exercised by Merrill Lynch[56]. So once again I was fired as a result of interference by the State Bar of Georgia.

The financial community in New York City is actually a small world so word spread rapidly about what had happened to me. The next day, I received a call from a friend at a large New England Life Agency located on the Avenue of the Americans in the city. This firm had a big office in New York City and I had done several large cases for them with Merrill Lynch clients. I went to see my friend and he took me into see the bossman. An hour later my wife and I were both working for New England Life.

We both worked long and hard to rebuild our client base in a city where we really didn't know a lot of people. As a result, we had to really work hard to sell insurance, no

---

[55] The mere fact that there was no hearing on the allegations, no trial, no service of process by Georgia was neither here nor there to Sensale. He could re-establish his reputation as never losing. I had to be guilty or why would the State Bar say these things. Suppose Mr. Sensale had been accused – would he have wanted people to be so flippant with his rights and his career?

[56] I still have the certificate guaranteeing me a $100,000.00 bonus if I stayed for ten years. If not for Paul B. Cohen I would have stayed. I was happy.

longer did we have the assistance of all of the stock brokers who wanted to diversify their client's portfolio's[57].

Well, I was tired of continually being slammed by the Georgia Bar and Paul Cohen so I called the State Bar of Georgia and asked what I had to do to be re-admitted. I was told by a young lady that in regard to my case, the State Bar would fight to the end to deny me re-admission. I asked why this attitude and was told that was just the way it was. Later this attitude was changed so that if I got 100 attorneys to sign a petition they would at least consider my readmission, but no guarantees.

Based on this attitude by the State Bar of Georgia I went to see the head of the American Civil Liberties Union in New York. I was sure that this was the type of case they would jump on. I got the shock of my life. When I asked them for help, he responded that while he agreed that I had been discriminated against, they didn't want to waste their money on a case like mine as they could not get enough bang for their buck since I was a white male and a veteran to boot.

---

[57] Though I had very good relationships with a number of stock brokers at Merrill Lynch, I was told that Sensale had told them all, on pain of immediately termination, to have nothing to do with me. I would hate to think he did not have an open mind about me.

Now if I had been a Black, pregnant female, or an illegal alien or some other minority they would be happy to help. But otherwise, no.

Since this mess had started with me trying to help a Black family, I went to the NAACP to see if they could help. I was not surprised that they would not even give me the time of day. I was white, don't you know.

I had to make a business trip to New Mexico and ran into a member of the Office of General Counsel of the State Bar of New Mexico. Out of sheer frustration, I told him the situation. His response surprised me. He said that if what I said was true about there being no hearing and I could prove it, then New Mexico would establish a panel to review the evidence. If I passed the Bar Exam and there had been no due process in Georgia in regard to what they had done, I would be admitted in New Mexico to practice. The only catch was that I had to be a New Mexico resident.

When I got back to New York, I discussed this matter with my wife. I knew that she was happy in the City and loved living at Trump Tower[58]. To my surprise, she did

---

[58] Over the course of the 2 or so years we lived there I had numerous contacts with Donald Trump. I found him to be a man of integrity and from listening to the employees talk, he was a very fair employer. Most of the allegations I have heard in the news are made up, especially the one by the lady who said he groped her outside the elevators in Trump Tower. Could not have happened, he always had a bodyguard with him.

not hesitate and said that if I could be reinstated in New Mexico then by all means let us go. The sooner, the better.

The next day I discussed the matter with our boss. He was understanding to a point, but when he found out that our plans included returning to New Mexico permanently, he was less than enthused. I represented a sizeable monetary value to he and his firm. Finally, he said something that I found supremely insulting and I got up and left. I have never set foot back in that office[59].

---

[59] I applied to take the February 1994 Bar Exam in November 1993. In my Application for Admission I included a full outlined of my status in regard to the State Bar of Georgia. Nothing was said to me regarding a problem with being admitted as a New Mexico Attorney if I passed the exam.

I even went so far as to meet with Lawrence Ramirez, Attorney and head of the State Bar Disciplinary Committee. This meeting was arranged by Richard Breazell and Rudy Ramirez, a relative of Mr. Lawrence Ramirez. After hearing the story, Mr. Ramirez told me that if I passed the exam, he saw no problem with my admission. Mr. Ramirez later contacted Mr. Breazell and informed him I was to be sworn in on or about June 5, 1994 and to make sure my move back to New Mexico was complete by the end of May. Mr. Ramirez lied.

WHY WOULD THEY SAY IT

CHAPTER SIX
ETHICS, YOU CAN'T EAT THEM

Eons ago, when I was in law school, and thought that the law really meant something, the law school I attended paid a sizeable fee to have a very prominent attorney to come lecture on ethics. We arrived in class ready to take copious notes on the mysterious world of legal ethics. However, he was sitting on the rostrum reading the newspaper. Ten minutes into class, he was still reading the paper. Finally, he folded the paper, took off his reading glasses, carefully returned them to his pocket and looked out at the class. He finally said something that I found very profound.

"Ethics, you can't eat them." At this point, he got up and left the classroom. Such was our lecture on legal ethics for the day. We all took something different away from that class that day.

Looking back, I am sorry to say that I was somewhat naive. I had been raised in a household where your word was your bond. I was from Tennessee, part of the Confederacy, but sort of borderline. I grew up associating with many people of all colors. I was partly raised by a part time Black nanny who was also my grandmother's housekeeper. To me, people were and are just simply people. So I was unprepared for what I discovered as an attorney.

As an Army Officer, I was also trained that my word was my bond. I took an oath to support and defend the constitution and a similar one when I was sworn in as an attorney. I was just simply not expecting to find so many out and out crooks in the bar or the judiciary. To my everlasting dismay, as I defended crooks and disreputable reprobates, I often discovered that the worst crooks were sitting on the bench.

Such is a sign of the times when the protections guaranteed us under the U.S. Constitution are viewed as interfering with making cases[60]. I met those with similar ethics in New Mexico when I applied to take the Bar Exam.

I gave full details about what happened in Georgia to the New Mexico Bar and stood ready to answer any

---

[60] I guess I should not have been surprised when I asked an Assistant U.S. Attorney how he could support using forged evidence in a trial. I asked where the justice was in that. His response was that he was not there to see justice done but to win cases. He would do whatever he needed to do to win. Is this what the law is all about?

questions. As was to be expected, the Office of General Counsel of the State Bar of Georgia had their usual fit when my name came up in a request for information by the State Bar of New Mexico.

According to the Rules of the State Bar of New Mexico, the State Bar of New Mexico appointed a panel of several attorneys to hear the evidence I would present and review what had been done by the State Bar of Georgia. Supposedly, if it was determined by this panel that there was no due process afforded me in what was done by the State Bar of Georgia, then it would be recommended that I be admitted to practice in New Mexico.[61]

The man appointed by the State Bar of New Mexico to be the chair of the panel and to also serve as the independent investigator was named C. Barry Crutchfield. He gave me this really good speech about getting to the truth – unfortunately it was all talk. It was later clear that C. Barry Crutchfield walked into that panel with his mind already made up. He also made a slip that left his ethics showing. Of course, the State Bar of New Mexico almost had a collective hernia trying to cover up for him.

---

[61] Now I had little respect for the State Bar of Georgia based on what had happened thus far, but even I had no idea how far they would go to ensure that I not be admitted to practice anywhere in the free world.

A logical starting point in regard to this review would be determining what the law has defined as Due Process of Law. Based upon what the U.S. Supreme Court has determined is due process of law, if the State Bar of Georgia did not afford that to me then there was no due process of law and I would be admitted. Once again, I was naïve, I thought these people involved in the governing of the State of New Mexico and the operation of the State Bar were people of their words. Not so. Before we were finished it was like something out of a Clive Cussler or John Grisham novel.

On April 9, 1994, while house hunting in Las Cruces, I had a telephone conversation with C. Barry Crutchfield wherein he assured me that he would get to the truth of the matter even he had to go to Georgia and personally investigate what had happened. I made the call to Mr. Crutchfield from Mr. Breazell's house and, through the use of a speaker phone, Mr. Breazell heard Mr. Crutchfield promise to thoroughly investigate my claims of violation of due process by Georgia to include going there.

At Mr. Crutchfield's urging, on April 20, 1994 I filed suit against Georgia in Federal Court in order to try and get a decision regarding the lack of due process. He had also recommended that I file against New Mexico in order to ensure that any decision rendered in my favor would be binding on New Mexico as well.

David McNeill was appointed to represent the New Mexico Board of Bar Examiners in Federal Court. On June 20, 1994 I received a letter from David McNeill that Mr. Crutchfield had completed his investigation and that a decision had already been made. I requested a hearing and heard nothing.

Finally, on July 25, 1994, I received written confirmation from Mr. Crutchfield that a hearing was scheduled for July 29, 1994. The members of this hearing were C. Barry Crutchfield chair, Henry Narvaez and Martha Daly, an attorney from AG Udall's staff. The hearing was stopped by Mr. Crutchfield and Mr. Narvaez in order to obtain some records and to have additional witnesses present. The hearing was to be reconvened by conference call later. This never happened.

In August, 1994, my wife discovered that C. Barry Crutchfield had been serving as local counsel for the Georgia Defendants without my knowledge. Mr. Crutchfield recused himself when confronted.

Mr. Narvaez proposed to hold a new hearing replacing merely one member, I declined and asked to go before the Court rather than this sham of a hearing. My response was ignored and a ruling entered against me which was contrary to the evidence presented.

I filed a complaint with the U.S. Attorney in Albuquerque but it was blocked by Presiliano Torrez, Assistant U.S. Attorney for Las Cruces and President of the Board of Bar Examiners. I filed a complaint with the Office of the New Mexico Attorney General, but it was declined. Martha Daly, a member of the panel, was a member of State Attorney General Tom Udall's staff.

So I had done as Crutchfield advised and sued the State of Georgia and the State of New Mexico in Federal Court. On the one hand, it was held against me by the State Bar of New Mexico, and caused some attorneys who were supporting my case to turn their back on me but on the other hand[62], I found out somethings that I could never have found out any other way. The Office of the General Counsel of the State Bar of Georgia had a spy in the New Mexico Bar. His identity was a shock to us all.

---

[62] From what was said later, it was Crutchfield's intent to have me held in disfavor by the State Bar of New Mexico.

CHAPTER SEVEN
JUSTICE IN NEW MEXICO

Merriam-Webster defines the word justice as being the quality of being just, impartial or fair or the principle or ideal of just dealing or right action. We expect those we appoint or elect to positions of trust to be fair and impartial in their decisions. I expected it of those administering the State Bar of New Mexico. In addition to the issues I had fought with the State Bar of Georgia, I discovered that I also had to fight racial bigotry in New Mexico. It was certainly disheartening.

If the reader will recall, in the previous chapter I discussed how C. Barry Crutchfield had urged me to file suit against both the State of New Mexico and the State of Georgia in regard to the findings of his panel. As in most things, my wife helped me with the paper work and went to the federal court house to file most of it. I believe that I had mentioned earlier that she had never met a stranger. So it was that she made a friend of the Court Clerk. One afternoon when she went to file some papers for me, she asked the clerk could she see the court file. Obligingly, the Clerk gave her the file and left her to review it.

What she found was a major revelation and shocked the hell out of me. She was allowed to make copies of these documents and brought them home to me. According to what she found, the State Bar of Georgia had secretly hired C. Barry Crutchfield[63] to represent their interests against me in regard to both the panel and the federal court case[64].

A Georgia attorney by the name of Robert Goldstucker was working with him. In other words, he secretly had been bribed to be a spy[65] and to protect the interests of the State Bar of Georgia from being revealed as denying due process of law to me.

I went ballistic, called the State Bar of New Mexico and reported the matter and then confronted Crutchfield. He of course denied it and no one at the State Bar of New Mexico seemed particularly concerned about a little thing

---

[63] **Exhibit A** – Notice of appearance signed by C. Barry Crutchfield representing Georgia from the Federal Case File.

[64] **Exhibit B** – A letter from C. Barry Crutchfield to the Office of General Counsel of the State Bar of Georgia confirming he was their representative in New Mexico.

[65] **Exhibit C** – Sworn discovery responses prepared by C. Barry Crutchfield where he admitted that he represented Georgia at the same time he was the Chair and Independent Investigator for the Panel to determine if I received due process form the State Bar of Georgia.

like a conflict of interest, after all I was just a tiresome gringo, not a fine upstanding member of society such as an attorney[66].

This of course called into question anything that the panel did and one of the members of the panel was a member of the staff of the State Attorney General (now U.S. Senator), Tom Udall. Mr. Udall was a friend of my wife's, so she went to see him. Though he was clearly busy, he heard her out and said that he would appoint an investigator and get to the bottom of the matter.

A few days later, this investigator, another member of his staff, appointed by Tom Udall called me at home and chewed me out for daring to make allegations against her best friend, Martha Daly. She went on to say that the young lady sitting on the panel was the most ethical attorney who had ever lived and it was reprehensible that I would say anything against her.

---

[66] **Exhibit B** - Someone at the State Bar of Georgia apparently decided that their criminal machinations should come to light and faxed a copy of a letter Mr. Crutchfield sent to the William P. Smith, III, then the General Counsel of the State Bar of Georgia, agreeing to secretly work for them. When I raised the issue of forgery in regard to the alleged resignation I am supposed to have signed, Crutchfield sneered that he thought that defense was ludicrous and the court agreed with him with no evidence. Naturally when the letter he sent came to light, the first thing he did was claim it was a forgery, not so ludicrous now.

I asked if she was going to investigate the matter and she said definitely not as it was her best friend and Tom Udall had told her to bury this matter. She also said if I knew what was good for me I would drop it[67]. So here was a member of Tom Udall's staff admitting that he had authorized a cover-up to bury the violations of my right to due process of law. Now that he is a fine upstanding United States Senator, I wonder what other cover ups he has authorized.

The next day I went to the office of the Assistant U.S. Attorney in Las Cruces, New Mexico. The Assistant Attorney General was a man by the name of Presiliano Torrez. Rather than let me into his office, he met us in the lobby of his office. When I told him what had happened, he frowned and said in front of witnesses:

"I don't care what they did, this is New Mexico, this is our Bar and if we don't want to let you in we do not have to. You people[68] need to learn we control here, not you."

With that he went back into his office and slammed the door behind him[69]. I reported the matter to the U.S.

---

[67] She was clearly young and naïve herself admitting such things without knowing if the line was recorded or not. I must say that the full conversation makes for interesting listening.

[68] In Georgia, the phrase "You People" automatically gets people to thinking about discrimination. But as I learned from the Obama Justice Department, white males have no rights under the law.

Attorney for New Mexico and never even received a response.

Needless to say, Crutchfield's influence resulted in the panel finding that I did receive due process in Georgia. To see how ridiculous this finding was, let's do something that the panel failed to do – look to see what the definition of due process of law is as decided by the U.S. Supreme Court.

Under our legal system there are two types of due process, substantive and procedural. The U.S. Supreme Court has very clearly stated that due process is the legal requirement that the state must respect all legal rights that are owed to a person. Due process balances the power of law of the land and protects the individual person from it.

When a government harms a person without following the exact course of the law, this constitutes a due process violation, which offends the rule of law. In this regard we need to look only at what procedural due process I was entitled to when the State Bar of Georgia sought to strip me of my right to practice law.

---

[69] Had I dared say such a thing to him I would have been in front of a federal judge before the day was out. But no one cared what he said or did since he was not a white male, but a fine upstanding member of the Bar while I was one of those trashy white males in his eyes.

Procedural due process is a legal doctrine in the United States that requires government officials to follow fair procedures before depriving a person of life, liberty, or property. When the government seeks to deprive a person of one of those interests, procedural due process minimally requires for the government to afford the person <u>notice</u>, an <u>opportunity to be heard</u>, and a decision made by <u>a neutral decision maker</u>.

Procedural due process is required by the Due Process Clauses of the Fifth and Fourteenth Amendments to the United States Constitution.

The article "*Some Kind of Hearing*" written by Judge Henry Friendly created a list of basic due process rights "that remains highly influential, as to both content and relative priority[70]". These rights, which apply equally to civil due process and criminal due process, are:

- An unbiased tribunal.
- Notice of the proposed action and the grounds asserted for it.
- Opportunity to present reasons why the proposed action should not be taken.

---

[70] Strauss, Peter. "DUE PROCESS". Legal Information Institute. Retrieved 8 March 2013.

- The right to present evidence, including the right to call witnesses.
- The right to know opposing evidence.
- The right to cross-examine adverse witnesses.
- A decision based exclusively on the evidence presented.
- Opportunity to be represented by counsel.
- Requirement that the tribunal prepare a record of the evidence presented.
- Requirement that the tribunal prepare written findings of fact and reasons for its decision.

Not all the above rights are guaranteed in every instance when the government seeks to deprive a person life, liberty, or property. At minimum, a person is due only notice, an opportunity to be heard, and a decision by a neutral decision maker[71].

I received none of these so how could anyone in their right mind decide that I had received due process of law from the State Bar of Georgia? Well, based on the evidence it appears that the panel was unduly influenced to make a decision not in keeping with the law, but in keeping with the desires of the powers that be.

---

[71] Except for me of course.

Crutchfield's replacement as chair of the panel proposed to just continue ahead to a decision. Normally, I would submit, when a member of a jury, or the judge, in this case, is found to be biased, the jury is sometimes replaced. When I raised the issue of Crutchfield's actions having poisoned the panel so to speak, the New Mexico Bar ignored me. In fact, I was attacked for daring to even insinuate that the New Mexico Bar might be unfair.

I was introduced to Manuel Lujan, a former member of President Reagan's cabinet. He mentioned that he had heard I had a problem and I told him my situation. He promised to make some inquiries. He later told me that he had been informed that if he helped me, a relative, who was in prison on trumped up charges would suffer. Lujan did get a promise out of "the powers that be" that if Georgia agreed I would be immediately admitted. He told me that the word had come down, I would not be admitted under any circumstances. I had to be taught a lesson.

CHAPTER EIGHT
I GO ON THE OFFENSIVE

Once it was clear that the State Bar of New Mexico and the State Bar of Georgia were working in concert, even if unofficially, I was forced to explore other options.

Under New Mexico law, I filed a claim against the state of New Mexico. I filed the claim with the Risk Management Department of the New Mexico State Government. The investigative firm hired by the State of New Mexico was called SOARS[72]. The investigator was a gentleman by the name of Roland Swanson.

I patiently waited for the findings of this investigation but apparently those entities contacted by the State Bar of Georgia were on the move. One evening I

---

[72] I later discovered that SOARS shared office space with William F. Riordan, the Defense Attorney in my State Case, the former Chief Justice of the New Mexico State Supreme Court and a man with a long standing professional relationship with the Judge in my state case. What could go wrong?

received a telephone call from Roland Swanson, the SOARS investigator. He asked me to meet him at a hotel on the outskirts of Las Cruces, but to not tell anyone that I was meeting him. I insisted that I bring my wife, as I sensed that I needed a witnesses. Mr. Swanson was very clearly nervous about meeting me and insisted that we go into a sheltered corner of the hotel lobby for our talk.

He admitted that after concluding his investigation which he said was quite thorough, he determined that there were several major ethical violations committed by the New Mexico State Bar and the panel chaired by C. Barry Crutchfield. In fact, he went on to say that his investigation showed that everything I had said was correct. I asked for a copy of the report but he said that since it was paid for by New Mexico, he could not give me a copy. I would have to subpoena it but he wanted me to know what he had found so it could not be hidden from me[73].

---

[73] Of course it really did not do me any good to know what was in the report as the State of New Mexico suppressed the report. In spite of everything that had taken place from bribery to denial of due process of law, I received the letter at **Exhibit D** that no wrong doing on the part of anyone in New Mexico was found. Of course, the signer of that letter, Betty J. McManaman had no idea what she was talking about. I did not bring a claim against the State Bar Examiner, but rather the State Bar and, as a matter of law, I could not be disbarred in Georgia without the hearing the State of Georgia refused to allow me to have. A suspicious person would think the fix was in.

The upshot was that in the Federal case I had filed, the State Bar of New Mexico had lied to the Court[74] and Mr. McNeill had committed several instances of ex-parte communication with the U.S. Magistrate which resulted in a general stay being entered in the case over my objections and with no legal basis. After a few more conversations between McNeil and the Magistrate the case was later dismissed[75].

I prepared a Time Table that shows what took place in regard to this panel[76]. One question was when did Crutchfield's secret representation of the State Bar of Georgia begin and end and when he made the decision that I had received due process from the State Bar of Georgia.

Based on Mr. Crutchfield's Response to my Request for Admissions and Interrogatories, as can be seen from his sworn responses, he made his decision that I had received due process from the State Bar of Georgia and should not be admitted to the State Bar of New Mexico

---

[74] This is called fraud on the court and has no statute of limitations. This is when the machinery of the court is interfered with. When attorneys lie, this is fraud on the court.

[75] I continued for over 17 years to request the report submitted to the State of New Mexico Risk Management by Roland Swanson. I was continually rebuffed until there was a change of personnel and Tim Korte sent me an email that the report had been destroyed at the end of 7 years. The email is at **Exhibit E.**

[76] **Exhibit F** – Time Table

prior to April 20, 1994. He then recused himself as investigator and panel chair prior to June 12, 1994 so that he could properly be Georgia's attorney from June 13 to June 20, 1994. He then again served as chair of the Panel in July of 1994. Apparently Crutchfield's ability to read a calendar changes based on his needs[77].

In the suit that I filed in State District court about the actions of the panel, the attorney for the Defendants (William F. Riordan[78]) also served as attorney for a witness who was properly subpoenaed by me for a deposition. The witness in question was the individual who was in charge of the records for the State of New Mexico. He was properly served with a subpoena duces tecum that was properly issued by the court. Riordan instructed the witness not to appear for the deposition in spite of a properly issued and served subpoena, certainly fraud on the court.

I moved for a hearing to have the witness held in contempt for failing to appear for the deposition and Riordan for telling his client to ignore a subpoena. As soon

---

[77] **Exhibit B** - On April 14, 1994, C. Barry Crutchfield wrote a letter to William P. Smith III, then General Counsel for the State Bar of Georgia confirming his agreement to represent the State Bar of Georgia and his agreement to influence the decision against me.

[78] He also represented C. Barry Crutchfield and anyone else who was even remotely a party or a witness. Conflict of interest? Certainly, but according to the Judge, Robert E. Robles, Riordan was so ethical it did not matter.

as the hearing started, Riordan jumped to his feet and demanded that the judge quash his own subpoena in the interests of justice. Without giving me a chance to speak, the Judge granted his request and refused to discuss why he did that[79].

Riordan then claimed for his clients the protection allowed for state agencies, after claiming the State Bar of New Mexico was a state agency and upon his request I was denied the opportunity to conduct discovery[80].

My case was then dismissed based upon sovereign immunity, a concept that was abolished in New Mexico in 1975[81], and res judicata and collateral estoppel even though the Judge admitted the issues in this case are not the same as in the Federal Case and also agreed that I never received a hearing in the Federal Court. In spite of that he felt I had

---

[79] The SOARS report was never released to me and when I tried again years later was told it had been destroyed shortly after it was submitted to them. So much for justice. I later learned that Riordan and Judge Robles had a long standing relationship. I was later told that Riordan had helped Judge Robles get a federal judgeship. The DA, Susana Martinez did not care, she's now Governor.

[80] It was not a state agency but an arm of the State Supreme Court, however, it was made clear to me that the State of New Mexico had to be protected from people like me.

[81] My ability to sue Georgia was reconfirmed by the United States Supreme Court in **Nevada v. Hall**, 440 U.S. 410 (1979). In this case the High Court held that a State is not constitutionally immune from suit in the courts of another State.

received due process by just being allowed to file the case. He just wanted the matter to end[82].

In response to my allegations of Crutchfield having a conflict of interest secretly representing the State Bar of Georgia while publicly serving as the chair and investigator of the panel that was to determine if I received due process of law from the State Bar of Georgia, the Judge said something so incredibly stupid that I was speechless. He said that *I had to understand that some people's ethics were so high he could represent both sides of a situation and what he knew on one side would not affect what he knew on the other side nor how he ruled.*

I went to the District Attorney in Las Cruces, New Mexico for help in regard to this blatant denial of due process of law. But the hard charging DA in this town was none other than Susana Martinez, now Governor of New Mexico. She had her sights set on higher political office and could not afford to be seen to side with a gringo against the powers that be in New Mexico. After she became Governor she appointed an attorney to be a special prosecutor to look into judicial corruption in the state. However, when I brought this case to him, he refused to

---

[82] Once again the concept of judicial discretion played a large role. These were his friends I was asking him to rule against. The good old boy system went into high gear to protect them.

discuss it. As I was learning, justice in New Mexico had a Hispanic face.

I later heard that this judge in my case received an appointment to the federal bench. Gives you a warm fuzzy feeling inside to know that such legal scholars hear your case.

CHAPTER NINE
JURISDICTION, WE DON'T NEED NO
STINKING JURISDICTION

At this point I think it would be beneficial to pick back up with the story of what happened in the State of Georgia. I am sure that by this time, the reader is wondering what I did in Georgia that was so horrible that the State Bar of Georgia has pursued me through California, New York, New Mexico and now Texas. What crime was so heinous that they bribe officials in other states to ruin me. Well, I will tell you – I refused to resign as a member of the State Bar of Georgia[83].

In 1990, a friend of mine in California asked me why I had been disbarred in the state of Georgia. When I heard this I was baffled as I had not been disbarred. In fact,

---

[83] I need to make the reader aware of an important point at this stage of the tale – State Courts and Federal District Courts must follow decisions of their respective Appellate Courts and all Courts must follow decisions of the U.S. Supreme Court under the supremacy clause of the U.S. Constitution.

the State Bar of Georgia was legally prohibited from having me disbarred by Georgia State Law without at least offering me hearing. To date no hearing has been offered.

Well, it seems that the Supreme Court of the State of Georgia accepted my resignation and based on the recommendation of the State Bar, literally revoked my license to practice law not only in that state but nationally. The only problem with that is that I had not submitted the resignation in question.

I called Paul B. Cohen, Assistant General Counsel of the State Bar of Georgia and asked him about this resignation. He assured me that I had submitted a resignation. When I told him that I had not signed, nor submitted a resignation, he laughed and said, *"well we have a signature and that is all that counts."* I asked for him to send me a copy, but it was over two years later before I ever saw a copy. It turns out that the State Bar of Georgia had written a nice little administrative law that allowed them to strip me of my right to due process of law without bothering the courts.

Once I did get a copy of the so-called resignation, I was shocked to see that it was multiple pages of me allegedly admitting to the commission of crimes. The signature was not notarized, nor witnessed and did not even look like mine. I asked Paul Cohen who had written this thing and he said that I had, since I had signed it[84]. It was also Paul B. Cohen who has assured the State Supreme Court of Georgia that I had signed the document. Everything had been done all nice and legally, EXCEPT, for those pesky things called Constitutional Rights.

The State Bar of Georgia submitted the matter to the State Supreme Court of Georgia recommending that my resignation be accepted. The Court accepted the recommendation, but never laid eyes on the so called resignation. The working of the decision of the State Supreme Court makes it clear this is what happened[85].

There is only one problem with what happened. None of it was legal. The State Supreme Court was without jurisdiction to even hear the matter, let alone render a decision[86].

First, under the provisions of Georgia Code Annotated, Section 15-19-32 it states:

- *"Rules and regulations governing the Unified State Bar shall provide that before a*

---

[84] I later obtained evidence that Paul B. Cohen, himself, had written the document in question.

[85] **EXHIBIT G**– Decision rendered by the Supreme Court of the State of Georgia.

[86] This was a wink, wink, nudge, nudge proceeding.

final order of any nature or any judgment of disbarment is entered, the attorney involved may elect to have any material issue of fact determined by a jury in the county of his residence."

I was never made aware of the fact that:

1. That I was entitled to a hearing,
2. That the document called my resignation would be used to create a special class called tantamount to disbarment,
3. That there was even going to be an attempt to disbar me.
4. What the charges against me consisted of,
5. That I had the right to be present and defend myself.

I had no idea any of this was in the works. Now the State Bar of Georgia took these actions in 1989. The position of the State Bar was that the state allowed me to practice law at the pleasure of the state and it could be revoked anytime and I literally had no rights.

However, the United States Supreme Court decided in 1971[87] that accused attorneys were entitled to the same protections as criminal defendants. The State Bar of

---

[87] **Geiger v. Jenkins**, 401 U.S. 985 (1971)

Georgia laughed at the very idea that I had any rights at all. Since the original case was brought in the Northern District of Georgia the State Bar should have been aware of it, but ignored the holding[88]. However, the Supremacy Clause of the United States Constitution clearly states that the opinion of the United States Supreme Court is paramount over the opinion of any state supreme Court.

In spite of the U.S. Constitution, the Supreme Court of the State of Georgia took the position that they were the final arbiter of all matters relating to the State Bar of Georgia under some ethereal inherent right to regulate the Bar and the provisions of Georgia Code Annotated, Section 15-19-30 which states as follows:

- *"In recognition of the fact that attorneys are officers of the courts of this state; that they have the exclusive right to practice law and represent members of the public in connection with their legal affairs; that they are charged with important responsibilities in connection with the administration of*

---

[88] This was a case involving an action to revoke the license of a doctor to practice. The trial court held that the state proceedings were in the nature of criminal proceedings. The U.S. Supreme Court affirmed the decision, which meant the State Bar of Georgia was bound by that decision.

justice both in and out of the courts; and that for these reasons a strong legal profession is in the public interest, the Supreme Court of this state is authorized to establish as an administrative arm of the court a unified self-governing bar association which shall be known as the "State Bar of Georgia," composed of all persons licensed to practice law in this state. (Ga. L. 1963, page 70, Section 1.)

Based on this statute, though the State Constitution was clear they had no original jurisdiction, the Supreme Court of the State of Georgia decided that they had the power to make judicial rulings regarding such matters as my alleged resignation. However, as a matter of law this statute could not confer jurisdiction to the court to hear my proceeding or any proceeding of this nature.

Jurisdiction is defined as the power of a court to adjudicate cases and issue orders or the Territory within which a court or government agency may properly exercise its power[89].

One of the most fundamental questions of law is whether a given court has jurisdiction to preside over a

---

[89] Ruhrgas AG v. Marathon Oil Co. et al., 526 U.S. 574 (1999).

given case. A jurisdictional question may be broken down into three components:

- whether there is jurisdiction over the person (in personam),

- whether there is jurisdiction over the subject matter, or res (in rem), and

- whether there is jurisdiction to render the particular judgment sought.

Lacking any of the three, the Court may not make a ruling as a matter of law. The term jurisdiction is really synonymous with the word "power". *Any court possesses jurisdiction over matters only to the extent granted to it by the Constitution, or legislation of the sovereignty on behalf of which it functions.* *The question of whether a given court has the power to determine a jurisdictional question is itself a jurisdictional question. Such a legal question is referred to as "jurisdiction to determine jurisdiction."*

Subject matter jurisdiction is the court's authority to decide the issue in controversy such as a contracts issue, or a civil rights issue. **State courts have general jurisdiction, meaning that they can hear any controversy except those prohibited by state law** (some states, for example, deny subject matter jurisdiction for a case that does not involve state citizens and did not take place in the state) and those allocated to federal courts of exclusive jurisdiction such as bankruptcy issues (see 28 U.S.C. § 1334). Federal courts have limited jurisdiction in that they can only hear cases that fall both within the scope defined by the Constitution in Article III Section 2 and federal statutes (See 28 U.S.C. §1251, §1253, §1331, §1332).

Territorial jurisdiction is the court's power to bind the parties to the action. This law determines the scope of federal and state court power. State court territorial jurisdiction is determined by the Due Process Clause of the Constitution's Fourteenth Amendment and the federal court territorial jurisdiction is determined by the Due Process Clause of the Constitution's Fifth Amendment.

Other forms of jurisdiction include appellate jurisdiction (the power of one court to correct the errors of another, lower court), concurrent jurisdiction (the notion that two courts might share the power to hear cases of the same type, arising in the same place), and diversity jurisdiction (the power of Federal courts to hear cases in which the parties are from different states)[90].

---

[90] Grupo Dataflux v. Atlas Global Group, L. P. (02-1689), 541 U.S. 567 (2004)

There was another problem with what the Supreme Court did in regard to my case. According to the 1983 Constitution of the State of Georgia, Article VI, Section VI, Paragraph 2:

Paragraph II. Exclusive appellate jurisdiction of Supreme Court. **The Supreme Court shall be a court of review and shall exercise exclusive appellate jurisdiction in the following cases:**

(1) All cases involving the construction of a treaty or of the Constitution of the State of Georgia or of the United States and all cases in which the constitutionality of a law, ordinance, or constitutional provision has been drawn in question; and

(2) All cases of election contest.

Paragraph III. General appellate jurisdiction of Supreme Court. Unless otherwise provided by law, the Supreme Court shall have appellate jurisdiction of the following classes of cases:

(1) Cases involving title to land;

(2) All equity cases;

(3) All cases involving wills;

(4) All habeas corpus cases;

(5) All cases involving extraordinary remedies;

(6) All divorce and alimony cases;

(7) All cases certified to it by the Court of Appeals; and

(8) All cases in which a sentence of death was imposed or could be imposed.

Review of all cases shall be as provided by law.

Questions:

1. **Did the Supreme Court of the State of Georgia have in Personam Jurisdiction (personal jurisdiction) over me**? The answer is no – I was living in the State of California at the time all of this was going on in Georgia. Since I was not under the area over which their jurisdiction extended there was no in rem jurisdiction. There was also no attempt to service with process to attempt to obtain in personam jurisdiction. The Court, therefore had no right to take any action against me.

2. **Did the Supreme Court of the State of Georgia have jurisdiction over the subject matter, or res (in rem)**, - The answer to this question is both yes and no. Under the above cited statute, the Court had jurisdiction over the Bar and how one became a member and could approve regulation on how one was removed. However, it did not have jurisdiction over the subject matter relating to me since it held a

hearing and issued a decision that removed my license without a hearing. and

3. **Did the Supreme Court have jurisdiction to render the particular judgment sought?** – It did not have any jurisdiction in this matter as a matter of State law as the State Constitution of Georgia stated very clearly that the Supreme Court of Georgia was to exercise **only** appellate jurisdiction.

It had no original jurisdiction to hear any matter, and yet it was acting as a court of original jurisdiction. So the State Supreme Court was without the power to hear the matter against me and by doing so made each justice liable for damages to my career. This was a very blatant attempt to punish a traitor to his race to keep other attorneys in line.

DUE PROCESS OF LAW

Much was said earlier about the right to due process of law. The right to due process of law is guaranteed to Americans by the 5th Amendment of the U.S. Constitution and the 14th Amendment to the U.S. Constitution. So what is the definition of Due Process of Law? The United States Supreme Court addressed this in a case entitled In Re

Murchison[91] wherein the High Court said very clearly that a fair trial in a fair tribunal is a basic requirement of due process. I never received a hearing, thus I never received due process. Unfortunately, the State Bar of New Mexico was unable to grasp this concept and found that I had received due process.

The Office of General Counsel of the State Bar of Georgia has long maintained that I signed the so called resignation. However, since I first was made aware of this so called resignation I have denied I signed it.

So what happens when there is forgery suspected in a legal case in Georgia? According to Georgia Code Annotated, Section 24-7-2:

- '*If a paper appears to have been altered materially, unless it is the paper sued on and no plea of NON EST FACTUM is filed, the party offering it in evidence shall explain the alteration, unless it comes from the custody of the opposite party.*

In other words, once I raised the issue of forgery, the Bar had the duty to prove it was a valid signature. They did not at the time and over 20 years later, have not. In fact,

---

[91]In Re Murchison 349 U.S. 133, 75 S.Ct. 623, 99 L.Ed 942.

WHY WOULD THEY SAY IT   /113

according to Georgia case law[92], when the alleged signer of a document at issue files a plea of NON EST FACTUM and denies signing the document, it falls to the party that wanted to use the document to prove it is valid.

I took the so-called resignation which was allegedly signed by me to a very well-known handwriting expert in New York City, Paul A. Osborn. In his report[93], Mr. Osborn specifically stated *"Studies of this reproduction at hand show some features which appear suspicious and could be the result of an imitation process as well as other features that would seem to be indicative of genuineness.*

A second handwriting examination was done in 2016 and it also said that it could not be said that I signed the document[94].

So what needed to be done? Georgia law is very clear on this issue as well. Once I raised the issue of forgery, Georgia Code Annotated, Section 24-7-6 is very clear.

§ 24-7-6. Proof of handwriting

Proof of handwriting may be resorted to in the absence of direct evidence of execution. In such case, any witness who

---

[92] **Diversified Growth Corp. v. Equitable Leasing**, 140 Ga. App. 511, 231 S.E.2nd 505.

[93] **Exhibit H** – Report of Paul Osborn, Forensic Document Examiner

[94] **Exhibit I** – Second Handwriting Examination by Susan Abbey, Forensic Document Examiner.,

shall swear that he knows or would recognize the handwriting shall be competent to testify as to his belief. The source of his knowledge shall be a question for investigation and shall go entirely to the credit and weight of his evidence.

However, no one knew me in the office of the State Bar of Georgia and thus no one could swear that it was my signature on that document. If the Bar is correct in its ravings I must have signed the document in California. The document is neither witnessed nor notarized. It was also claimed that since the document was in my Bar file, it had to be mine, Georgia law is clear on that point as well[95].

Therefore, under Georgia law, the so-called resignation was inadmissible before a court as a matter of law[96]. Thus the Bar merely told the court about it and submitted a recommendation that it be accepted. Hardly due process of law or following Georgia's own laws.

---

[95] Though the Bar seemed to feel if it was filed in my file it had to be mine, Georgia law maintains that even **POSSESSION NOT PROOF OF AUTHENTICITY.** --Proof that letters were found in the defendant's possession is not proof that the handwriting in the letters was his. McCombs v. State, 109 Ga. 496, 34 S.E. 1021 (1900).

[96] **HANDWRITING INADMISSIBLE WITHOUT PROOF.** --A writing, alleged to be in the handwriting or signature of a party, is inadmissible unless the writing is proved or acknowledged to be genuine. Gunter v. State, 243 Ga. 651, 256 S.E.2d 341 (1979).

In fact, the question of authenticity of any written document is a matter for the jury under Georgia law[97], but their short cut way of getting rid of me did not allow for a jury as the State Supreme Court did not and does not have the power to empanel a jury for any reason or be a trier of law. In my case, the State Supreme Court did not even see the document in question, but only accepted the recommendation of the State Bar.

To make it even more clear, the U.S. Supreme Court has gone on record regarding the rights of an attorney faced with disbarment[98]. **In Bradley v. Fisher**, 60 U.S. 335, 20 L.Ed 645 (1871) the high court held:

- *"In order to revoke or suspend the license of an attorney, the law requires that there should be an accusation and charges, a notice and a day in court, and **it cannot be done summarily by order of***

---

[97] **AUTHENTICITY IS QUESTION FOR JURY**. --A statement that the handwriting is that of a certain person is to be taken not as a conclusion but merely as an opinion the weight of which is a matter entirely for the jury. Borders v. City of Macon, 18 Ga. App. 333, 89 S.E. 451 (1916); Bates v. State, 18 Ga. App. 718, 90 S.E. 481 (1916); Rogers v. Rogers, 52 Ga. App. 548, 184 S.E. 404 (1936); Notis v. State, 84 Ga. App. 199, 65 S.E.2d 622 (1951); Gaulding v. Courts, 90 Ga. App. 472, 83 S.E.2d 288 (1954).

[98] I might make note of a peculiar position of the State Bar. At one point in the back and forth, Paul Cohen made the comment that I had not been disbarred, but that I had disbarred myself by resigning. By resigning I had forfeited all of my rights to due process. Apparently that applied only to me and no one else.

__the court.__ The law makes no difference between an attorney and other holding office during good behavior and other vested rights to be taken away by "due process of law," and __*requires in every case or proceeding to take away such an office, right or franchise, that the party shall have notice and opportunity to be heard, before the Court can acquire jurisdiction to adjudicate*__ *and that jurisdiction is limited to the exercise of a legal discretion by a court and does not include arbitrary acts of a judge."*

In my case, there was no notice, no charges, no service of process or opportunity to be heard. In fact, the State Supreme Court, in spite of its alleged inherent powers was prohibited from exercise original jurisdiction over any matter by the State Constitution and therefore, could not have empaneled a jury to hear the matter or determine the validity of the document.

It is interesting to note that William P. Smith III, General Counsel of the State Bar of Georgia at the time, responded to one of my filings by stating that there is no constitutional right to practice law and the State of Georgia could take it away from me at any time for any reason.

However, even in this he was wrong[99]. Maybe there is not one in the Republic of Georgia, but there is a constitutional right to practice law in this country.

In the case cited below, the **Supreme Court of New Hampshire v. Piper**, the U.S. Supreme Court clearly stated five years *before* the abortion I experienced that *the right to practice law is a "fundamental right" and therefore protected by the Fourteenth Amendment's Privileges and Immunities Clause of the U.S Constitution.* Apparently, the Supreme Court of Georgia has never heard of the Supremacy Clause. However, the rest of the country has. Therefore, as a matter of law, the fundamental right to practice law cannot legally be taken *from* me without a hearing and a right to be heard. I *received* neither.

In one of its responses, the State Bar of Georgia stated *"it is well settled that disbarment proceedings are not criminal in nature and that there is no constitutional right to practice law"*[100].

Whoever did the research for the State Bar of Georgia was either confused or just did not care. Cushway

---

[99] **Supreme Court of New Hampshire v. Piper**, 470 U.S. 274, 105 S. Ct. 1272, 84 L. Ed. 2d 205, 1985 U.S

[100] To support this position, the State bar of Georgia cited **Cushway v. State Bar of Georgia**, 120 Ga. App. 371 (1969) ; **Sams v. Olah**, 225 Ga. 497, 504 (1969) ; **Gordon v. Clinckscales**, 215 Ga. 843, 845 (1960).

v. State Bar of Georgia was decided in 1969; Sams v. Olah was decided in 1969 and Gordon v. Clinckscales was decided in 1960. Cases printed in the various legal reporters are normally cited as authority for various positions, how the law changes over time. Before citing a case printed in a legal reporter as good legal authority, there is a requirement that the case be Shepardized. There is a series of books called Shepard's Citations which gives the current state of the case in question. Lastly, these three cases do not even actually support the proposition that there is no constitutional right to practice law.

In regard to these three cases, as I pointed out earlier, they were overruled by the U.S. Supreme Court in 1985 by the U.S. Supreme Court in the holding in The Supreme Court of New Hampshire v. Piper that clearly stated that right to practice law is a "fundamental right" and therefore protected by the Fourteenth Amendment's Privileges and Immunities Clause of the U.S Constitution.

Instead of using good law, the State Bar of Georgia used overturned cases to support their position and none of the later courts really cared. The primary evidence used against me in each and every court was **"Why Would They Say It If It Wasn't True**.[101]**"**

It is interesting to note that in place of my Constitutionally protected right to due process of law, the State Bar of Georgia literally stripped me of my rights in order to protect a cabal of thieves highly placed thieves in the state legal system who are still fleecing their clients.

Currently, Federal Judges across the country are falling over themselves to protect the rights of immigrants who might want to come here. However, I as an American citizen are denied the rights I am currently and actually entitled to and no one cares. These same judges who stomp on their panties at the very idea that some poor person somewhere in the world might be denied some taxpayer funded benefit don't care that the law was broken in my case. I have sued the State Bar of Georgia twelve times and not had a meaningful hearing on the facts yet. In some of my cases the judges issue high sounding rhetoric and then,

---

[101] Frankly, true justice would be each person involved in the rendering of the decision against me and all of the later judges, federal and state who supported this decision and took part, knowingly or unknowingly in the ensuring cover-up should be suspended form the right to practice for as long as I have been.

when they cannot find fault with my legal arguments, use judicial discretion[102] to end the case.

In other cases, federal judges have ruled that they don't have jurisdiction to hear my case, but a judge in Hawaii can ban the President's executive order nationally because some immigrant, somewhere in the world might possibly want to come here to exercise his apparent Constitutional right to blow something up or kill American citizens.

Must I wait for every immigrant who wants to come here to be helped before I am entitled to have my rights protected? Apparently so.

Even when I show the court that the law was broken by the Georgia Bar, the judges have ignored it and dismissed the case. Where is the justice? If these judges are willing to ignore the law they have sworn to uphold, then what route does an individual have in order to get justice. I have had judges dare me to file complaints against them with the senior judges. However, in looking at the statistics for complaints filed against judges in the 13 circuits and 2

---

[102] Judicial discretion is the power of the judiciary to make some legal decisions according to their discretion. Under the doctrine of the separation of powers, the ability of judges to exercise discretion is an aspect of judicial independence. In other words, in spite of the law, they can use their opinion to decide cases which allows for some unbelievable coverups..

national courts from 1996 through 2008, 99.82% of complaints were dismissed without even an investigation. This is the good old boy system hard at work to protect the elite.

Now a couple of the judges were legal scholars and decided to shut me down once and for all. They pointed to Article IV, Section 2 of the United States Constitution. This is the "Full Faith and Credit Clause." This clause means that if one State had ruled on a matter, all of the rest of the states must abide by the decision. So I was informed that I was just out of luck.

However, in their enthusiasm to kick me out of court, these judicial scholars overlooked a few things. It seems that there are exceptions to this clause. The United States Supreme Court held in <u>Griffin v. Griffin</u>[103], a 1846 case that *a judgment obtained in violation of procedural due process is not entitled to full faith and credit when sued upon in another jurisdiction.*

In another U.S. Supreme Court decision, the court held that *a judgment rendered in violation of due process*

---

[103] **<u>Griffin v. Griffin</u>**, (1946) 327 U.S. 220, 90 L.Ed. 635, 66 S.Ct 556, REH DEN 328 U.S. 876, 90 L.Ed. 1645, 66 S.Ct. 975

is void in the rendering state and is not entitled to full faith and credit elsewhere[104].

In still another case discussing the full faith and credit clause, the U.S. Supreme Court, held[105] that *before this clause can become operative, one must have had his day in court, since it is of the essence of "due process of law" that one must be given an opportunity to be heard*[106].

Finally, in <u>Old Wayne Mutual L. Assoc. v. McDonough, Ind.</u>, a 1907 case, the U.S. Supreme Court held that this section (Article IV, Section 2 – The Full Faith and Credit Clause) is necessarily to be interpreted in connection with other provisions of the Constitution and therefore no State can obtain in the Tribunals of other jurisdictions, Full Faith and Credit for its judicial

---

[104] **World-wide Volkswagen Corp. v. Woodson** (1980) 444 U.S. 286, 62 L.Ed. 2d 490, 100 S.Ct. 559 [overruled on other grounds] Insurance Corp of Ireland, Ltd. V. Compagnie Des Bauxites De Guinee, 456 U.S. 694, 72 L.Ed. 2d 492, 102 S.Ct. 2009, 34 Fr Serv 2d, [Later proceeding (W.D. Pa.] 554 F.Supp. 1080, Rev (Ca3d Pa) 724 F.2d 369 and later proceeding (W.D. Pa) 555 F.Supp. 1027, rev (Ca3Pa) 723 F.2d 357) As stated in Madison Consulting Group v. South Carolina (Ca 7 Wis) 752 F.2d 1193.

[105] **Pink v. AAA Highway Express**, (1941) 13 S.E.2d 337, 191 Ga. 502, affirmed 62 S.Ct. 241, 314 U.S. 201, 86 L.Ed. 152, Rehearing denied 62 S.Ct. 477, 314 U.S. 716, 86 L.Ed. 570.

[106] Of course had I been given the opportunity to be heard, I would have been naming names. This could not be allowed.

proceedings if they are wanting in the due process of law[107].

In my case, what they are doing is protecting the judges and the state of Georgia from having to answer for their wrongdoing as well as other judges, both federal and state from having to answer for violating my rights.

So I must ask if a judge knowingly protects a wrongdoer, how is this different from Crutchfield secretly taking a bribe to protect the interests of the State Bar of Georgia. In both cases they are violating the oath they took when sworn in.

Now these judges and attorneys have all claimed at one time or another that all the parties (apparently to include the janitors in the Courthouses) to what happened are entitled to a good faith immunity and any and all judges have a sacred judicial immunity protected by GOD. The anointed ones of the federal bench will be quick to tell you they are appointed for life and can do as they please, law be damned. Judicial discretion is another name for I don't like the law and want to be in charge so we are going to do it my way.

---

[107] **Old Wayne Mutual L. Assoc. v. McDonough, Ind.**, 1907, 27 S.Ct. 236, 204 U.S. 8, 51 L.Ed. 345, See also Wetmore V. Kerrick, DC. 1907, 27 S.Ct. 434, 205 U.S., 141, 51 L.Ed. 745.

The good faith immunity (the Nuremberg Defense) was discussed by the United States Supreme Court in Wood v. Strickland[108] in 1975. In this case the Court held that *"an official is not immune if he (or she) knew or reasonably should have known that the action(s) . . . would violate . . . constitutional rights . . . or if he took the action with the malicious intention to cause a deprivation of constitutional rights or other injury."*

Now the immunity test was modified in 1982[109]. In the Harlow case, the court held that *"government officials performing discretionary functions are generally shielded from liability for civil damages insofar as their conduct does not violate clearly established statutory or constitutional rights of which a reasonable person would have known."*

All of the actors in Georgia knew or should have known what the law was in regard to my right to due process of law. I mean after all, they were the administrators of the State Bar of Georgia and the Justices of the State Supreme Court so it is hard to see how they would not have known that I was entitled to due process of law. Even a glance at the Constitution of the United States,

---

[108] **Wood v. Strickland**, 420 U.S. 308 (1975)
[109] **Harlow v. Fitzgerald**, 457 U.S. 800 (1982)

which they had sworn to support and defend would have given them a clue as to the constitutional rights I was entitled to. The due process of law afforded me was as follows:

- No notice of any charges,
- No service of process from any judicial body
- No notice of hearing
- No right to respond
- No hearing nor right of appeal
- No jury of my peers,
- Forged documents used against me.
- No personal jurisdiction
- No subject matter jurisdiction
- No legal court of original jurisdiction to hear the case.

Now Georgia may argue that it was a slight oversight they applied law that had been overruled. However, let's look at some other laws they ignored in their rush to protect the system from people like me.

The following U.S. Supreme Court decisions applied at the time;

Daniels v. Williams[110], and Davidson v. Cannon[111], held that *fair process is required for intentional actions of government or its employees*. I would submit that denying me any sort of due process was not fair process.

Leis v. Flynt[112] a 1979 case held that the right to due process guaranteed under the 5th Amendment does not create property or liberty interests, but instead provides that there are procedural safeguards against arbitrary deprivation.

This was Justice lite, or as I like to call it, the good old boy system at work. But boy has every court almost turned itself inside out to protect this wonderful due process they maintain I received.

However, for whatever reason[113], for over 25 years I have been denied any meaningful hearing into whether or not my rights were violated. Now if I was an illegal immigrant, I would have States Attorney Generals falling all over themselves to grandstand for the cameras to protect my rights. But alas, I am just an American citizen and a

---

[110] **Daniels v. Williams**, 474 U.S. 327 1986
[111] **Davidson v. Cannon**, 474 U.S. 344 (1986)
[112] **Leis v. Flynt**, 439 U.S. 438 (1979)
[113] Perhaps the protection of the good old boy system and the illegal income stream from the legal scams Judge Land informed me about would be good reasons.

veteran. I apparently have no rights or at least my rights rank well below those of potential terrorists.

To take it even further, as a direct result of the actions of the State Bar of Georgia I have lost significant job opportunities. They claim they are merely responding to requests for information when they tell people I have been disbarred. They do not tell those that enquire that a finding of disbarment in Georgia was prohibited absent a hearing. This way of continuing to screw me has also been addressed by the U.S. Supreme Court.

In **Paul v. Davis**[114], the U.S. Supreme Court held that *"while case law makes it clear that injury to reputation, in and of itself, is not a deprivation of liberty or property, there are cases that hold that if governmental actions (such as a statement of reasons given for termination of public employment) so injure a person's reputation that he will have lost significant employment or associational opportunities, there is a loss of liberty."*

Georgia has argued that there is not a property right involved. Once again, they are confused as to what the law is. **In Schwarz v. Board of Bar Examiners**[115] and

---

[114] **Paul v. Davis**, 424 U.S. 693 (1976)

[115] **Schwarz v. Board of Bar Examiners**, 353 U.S. 232, 77 S.Ct. 752, 1 L.Ed 2d 796 and **Konigsberg v. State Bar of California**, 353 U.S. 252, 77 S.Ct. 722, 1 L.Ed. 2d 810.

Konigsberg v. State Bar of California, the U.S. Supreme Court very clearly stated, *the right to practice law is a property right within the due process and equal protection provisions of the Fourteenth Amendment of the U.S. Constitution of the United States*. Nowhere in the terms of the Fourteenth Amendment does it exclude American citizens and veterans from equal protection of the law as I have been excluded.

No one in any court has looked at my rights. They have been more concerned with protecting the rights of the State of Georgia. I list in one of the Appendices all of these fine upstanding judges who do not understand what their job entails and those in Georgia who do not understand the law in general, not that I expect them to have to face any punishment for destroying my life, both personally as well as professionally. I can only wish them the same life I have been forced to live.

Of course the real shocker to me is what happened when I went to the extra-judicial organizations and reported the violation of the rights of the Black clients[116]. I have

---

[116] I might make note at this point that what really sent the State Bar of Georgia into a tailspin was when I went to the office of the U.S. Attorney in Atlanta and reported what was taking place and what I had been told. The Assistant U.S. Attorney that I discussed this matter with called the Office of General Counsel of the State Bar of Georgia and reported that I was not a team player.

already discussed the reaction of the ACLU and the NAACP when I reported the situation to them. They did not care, primarily because I am white. It made no difference those being screwed in Georgia were primarily Black or that I was punished for representing Blacks.

I also sent a written report on the fleecing of Black clients by these attorneys and Judges to both Reverend Al Sharpton and the Reverend Jesse Jackson[117]. Neither one did me the courtesy of responding or even looking into the matter. In spite of all of their high sounding rhetoric about protecting the rights of minorities, neither one gave me the time of day or checked to see if I was correct.

I send a full write-up to Black Lives Matter. They have marched and rioted all in the name of the rights of Blacks. However, when made aware of what are clearly violations of the rights of Blacks again there is no response. I guess there was not the opportunity to get some camera time for them and their alleged cause.

I sent a full write-up to the New York Times and the Atlanta Newspapers, the Governor of the State of Georgia, Governor Deal, the Office of the Attorney General of the State of Georgia and the Mayor of Columbus,

---

[117] I actually sent reports to these 2 gentlemen twice. One in the early 1990s and the second time a few months ago.

Georgia where this all took place. Again no response from anyone, except the Office of the Attorney General of Georgia to what should have been a front page story.

According to the Office of the Attorney General, they have no control over the actions of the State Bar of Georgia – I should report matters to the Mayor of Columbus who would or could tell the District Attorney who could, well, maybe do something. I guess the denial of due process to one attorney and the Black voters of the State of Georgia did not matter to the elected officials or the 4th estate. Maybe the public does not have a right to know.

After all of this I have to ask – DOES ANYONE CARE? The good old boy system even controls the law in Georgia. For not going along with what Judge Land wanted I was branded a traitor to my race and held up as an example of what happens if you fail to follow instructions. The point I want to make at this juncture is that if you control the members of the Bar (through fear if nothing else) you control the law in the State of Georgia.

CHAPTER TEN
TEXAS JUSTICE

For the last twenty years I have lived in the State of Texas. I have tried several times to get both State and Federal Judges here to issue ruling that the Full Faith and Credit Clause does not apply and that they issue rulings that the Georgia decisions not apply here due to lack of due process. I have been laughed at.

One imaginative federal Judge even went so far as to say that to inquire as to whether there was due process of law or not in the decision meant going behind the decision which is what the Full Faith and Credit Clause was meant to stop.

I must comment once again that while Federal Judges are currently saying they can make decisions that apply nationally, no one can do so in regard to the violation of my constitutional rights. I am an American veteran and clearly have less in the way of rights than illegal immigrants. Talk about an abuse of discretion.

Recently, I filed against the State Bar of Georgia based on their actions in another case I became involved in.

As I mentioned earlier, I am a 100% disabled veteran. Under Federal law I am entitled to a 10-point preference in applying for federal jobs. I applied for a public affairs position with the Department of Veterans Affairs. The interviewing official was a woman by the name of Marie Andrews.

When I went for the interview I found that she was the only interviewer present and some others were on a conference call link-up. Before the interview started, she said very aggressively that she did not like to work with men. Then during the interview, she made much about the fact that I had written a book widely used successfully by veterans who wanted to get their benefits.

At the time I had four degrees, including a law degree, and had served in a public affairs role for a major corporation that did government contracts. I was not selected because Marie Andrews felt I might side too much with the veterans and not with management.

We wound up going to federal court and I found that everyone and their dog was opposed to my having the job[118]. During the case, I underwent a deposition with the Assistant U.S. Attorney who hauled out a big stack of documents from the State Bar of Georgia. I was cross examined on each document, many of which I had never seen before and some which were not even signed. He maintained since I had been disbarred I could not pass a background check and thus could not have the job[119].

I responded that as a matter of law I could not be disbarred without a hearing and that I had been denied a hearing and the court that issued the ruling had no jurisdiction. His response was very telling about justice under the Obama administration.

Now remember this was an Assistant U.S. Attorney making the statement. I said it is hardly fair to cross examine me on documents that are not even signed and make accusations based on forged evidence. His response was **I DO NOT CARE ABOUT FAIR OR JUST. MY JOB IS TO WIN CASES ANY WAY I CAN.**

---

[118] I was later told by a friend working in VA personnel that under the new rules a disabled veteran who was hired got a year's sick leave in advance so supervisors did not know if the disabled veteran would be at work or not so no one wanted to hire them. A disabled veteran cannot be hired by the VA, who'd a thunk it.

[119] Of course, I never underwent a background check so we do not know for sure what would have happened.

I called the Justice Department and asked the Civil Rights Division about whether or not I could take advantage of the laws protecting disabled. The attorney said though I met the definition of disabled under the law since I was a white male, Attorney General Holder had said that white males had no rights under the civil rights laws. I was out in the cold again.

Well, no one's luck can be all bad. I was allowed to enter the Department of Veteran's Affairs Vocational Rehabilitation Program (VOCREHAB). I entered the Communication program at the University of Texas at El Paso (UTEP) to study digital media technology[120]. I was well aware that many of the professors were so liberal that they had trouble walking upright, but I make it a point to get along with everyone that I can.

I do not hide the fact that I am a veteran and a disabled one at that. In fact, I normally wore a hat that proclaimed to the world that I am a disabled veteran. Rarely has this been a problem. However, it became one at UTEP which was a decidedly anti-veteran university.

I finished the program with a 4.0 grade point average. I decided that I wanted to go for a Ph.D. in

---

[120] Learn how to make movies.

history[121] and VOCREHAB would have paid for it. Most Ph.D. candidates were on some kind of scholarship so it was rare for the student to offer to pay. To my shock, both the History Department and the University was opposed to my entering the Ph.D. program.

I went to see Dean Witherspoon who laughed at the very idea of me getting a more advanced degree[122]. I pointed out that I had a 4.0 GPA and she sneered at me that Communications was barely a degree. I went back to the Department Head who was amazed at my reception. He sent me to the office of the President who sent me to see the Campus Office which assisted the disabled.

I discovered that the University was keeping a secret file on me in order to justify not admitting me to the PH.D. program. There were allegations that I was out of control since a female student[123] I did not know had

---

[121] I had written at the time over 40 books many of them involving historical research. This was more than had been written by all of the professors at UTEP. It was also held against me that most of the books written by professors sold only because they were used as textbooks. Mine sold because people liked them.

[122] At one point I was told I was too (60) old and too stupid to get such a coveted degree.

[123] I was told her name was Maria Contreras and she apparently objected to my asking for a sleeping non-disabled student to be removed from a bench made available for disabled students. I am a 100% disabled veteran who walks with the aid of braces and a cane, but by asking to sit down, I was somehow being threatening.

allegedly filed a police report that I was threatening. I was denied the right to see it. Four years later I still have not been allowed to see it. It was shortly after this that I discovered this secret file being kept by the University regarding me.

On September 12, 2013 I filed a request under the Texas Public Information Act for a copy of all of the documents referenced in the secret file. To date I have not been given the requested documents.

On Tuesday, March 5, 2013 in response to an email sent to me by Manelic Alcala, Administrative Assistant at Center for Accommodations and Support Services (CASS) directing me to either call or come into the office to take part in an intake interview I presented myself at the CASS office. My name had been furnished to them by Cheryl B. Toursney, Senior Vice Provost for the University.

The head of this office, William (Bill) Dethlefs, Ph.D. apparently thought he was a shrink. Before he even met me, he sent an email to his boss that I was clearly *a Vietnam Veteran who was trained in combat and prone to violence.* This was all based on the hat that I wore and the fact that I was a veteran of the age to have been in Vietnam.

I reported in as directed by the email from CASS, however, my reception was anything but cordial. I was allowed to see Neelam Agarwal, Deputy Director, who informed me that she could not see me as she had a meeting. She was abrupt and impersonal, giving the attitude that I was bothering her. Based on this less than friendly reception I left.

It seems, based on the emails in the file that it was Neelam Agarwal's supervisor William Dethlefs who started and exacerbated the ensuing problems. As he makes clear in the email of March 5, 2013 from Bill Dethlefs to Gary Edens, Vice President for Student Affairs, and Catie McCorry-Andalis, Associate Vice President and Dean of Students for UTEP, Mr. Dethlefs has a preconceived idea about veterans in general as he stated *"we have had a more difficult time with veterans then with any other group. Many of these have also come before Ryan's Office due to their inappropriate behavior*[124]*."*

Even though I responded to an email from his office to call or drop in, by dropping in to his office, somehow I demonstrated inappropriate behavior that had to be reported up the chain.

I might also point out that this man prepared and disseminated a psychological diagnosis that I had a mental

---

[124] I objected to this stereotyping but was informed that it was not at issue since everyone knew that veterans were a threat and a potential terrorist as one attorney general had written.

problem, but can't get his facts straight in any of his emails regarding me. I left the CASS office after Ms. Agarwal told me that she had a meeting and could not see me, not before. It should also be noted that even though he is doing diagnosis which are being communicated up the chain and used by the University, William Dethlefs is not a licensed psychologist according to the Texas State Board of Examiners of Psychologists nor is he a licensed professional counselor according to the Texas State Board of Licensed Counselors. Thus he is not legally able to do either a medical or a mental diagnosis of anyone in the State of Texas and certainly not based on just two or three short meetings.

On Tuesday, April 16, 2013, as a disabled veteran, I asked Bill Dethlefs for the accommodation of having the door to classroom 403 in the Liberal Arts Building unlocked 15 minutes early so that I could sit down and he told me he thought it was a reasonable accommodation. Based on his statements to me, I was of the impression that it would not be a problem to have a classroom door opened fifteen minutes early. I heard nothing back from him to the contrary.

On April 16, 2013 I was denied entry to the classroom by a student employee by the name of Maria

Michel. She became incensed when I told her that CASS had said I was asking for a reasonable accommodation. She yelled she was going to tell the Dean and I told her to please do so.

I might also point out that the bench in that area referenced in her written statement was at that time and most times taken up by non-disabled students, studying, sleeping or just sitting waiting for class. There are no seats marked for disabled and the two seat bench referred to by Ms. Michel was occupied at the time by a sleeping non-disabled student. I was not told until April 17, 2013 that my request for accommodation had been denied.

I did not find out until the release of this secret file on September 11, 2013 that I had a serious mental problem. Bill Dethlefs had diagnosed me as *"having trouble adapting to college life"* and reported this diagnosis up the chain of the University as shown by the emails released to me from the secret file maintained by Ryan C. Holmes. Due to the secrecy that surrounded the diagnosis, I was not made aware of this diagnosis that I had a mental problem nor its reporting until I read it in the file.

This information was used, however, as the basis for calling me on the carpet by Ryan C. Holmes April 24,

2013 and being asked *"Are you a danger to yourself or others?"* I found the question highly offensive.

I might point out that although Mr. Holmes made me aware of the existence of the file in question; he refused to allow me to see it at the time. I might also point out that under the Family Education and Privacy Rights Act (20 United States Code) whenever a student has attained eighteen years of age, or is attending an institution of postsecondary education, the permission or consent required of and the rights accorded to the parents of the student shall thereafter only be required of and accorded to the student. So I was entitled to see those documents at the time I requested them, but due to my mental problem I was denied these documents.

I also believe that for Bill Dethlefs to arrive at a diagnosis that I had a mental problem[125] was highly improper and, since he was not unlicensed to make such diagnosis, illegal and a violation of my right of privacy as a minimum[126]. In fact, I am still not sure what his basis was for making such a diagnosis but he spread the information about it far and wide.

---

[125] (a diagnosis is defined as the act of identifying a disease, illness, or problem by examining someone or something or a statement or conclusion that describes the reason for a disease, illness, or problem.)

[126] However, UTEP covered for his violations since I was one of those nasty, dangerous out of control veterans.

He was not a medical doctor so he is not a psychiatrist. In the State of Texas Psychologists have PhDs or doctoral degrees (which he purports to have), have had supervised clinical hours, and have passed licensing exams. They can diagnose and treat mental illness. They cannot prescribe medication in Texas; however, they are increasingly allowed to prescribe medication in other states if they receive additional training. If properly qualified, they can testify about competency and sanity in criminal court. Psychologists use a variety of testing instruments to measure behavioral and psychological characteristics including memory, intelligence, personality disorders, psychosis, depression, ADHD, trauma exposure, aptitude for work, etc. However, this man had, at the time, worked at UTEP for almost 6 years, first with the Alumni Association and for the last 3 years Director of CASS. He was and as far as I know is not licensed as a psychologist and certainly conducted no tests before making his diagnosis and then passing it on to others.

These actions by Bill Dethlefs in notifying the administration of UTEP that I had a mental disorder amounted to Defamation of Character[127]: The tort of

---

[127] He apparently told campus security with would often show up to watch me. Witnesses have asked me what they usually had their hands

defamation of character consists of injury to another person's reputation, name, or character through spoken or written words for which damages can be recovered. Dethlefs' illegal diagnosis has certainly damaged my reputation, name and character within the University. I might make note that there are two kinds of defamation, libel and slander. Libel is false and malicious writing about another such as in published materials, pictures, and media[128].

Slander, which he committed when he discussed this diagnosis over the phone or in person, is false and malicious spoken words. Slander can be seen in the following comment directed by a patient toward the physician, "Dr. Woo is incompetent. He should have his license revoked." The statement is overheard by the office receptionist and other patients waiting in the reception area.

His secret examination of me upon which he based his diagnosis also constituted Invasion of Privacy, another kind of tort. It includes unauthorized publicity of patient information, medical records being released without the

---

on their guns when around me. It actually endangered my life, but no one cared since I was a nasty, dangerous veteran.

[128] Which he committed when he sent the emails about my mental problem to the administration.

patient's knowledge and permission, and patients receiving unwanted publicity and exposure to public view.

A second situation exists when persons other than those providing care and performing examinations and procedures (essential or nonessential personnel) are allowed to be present without the patient's consent. Yet another example is that the patient's right to privacy has been violated when asked to walk from the examination room across the hall to a treatment room while wearing only a patient gown in full view of other patients and personnel.

There is no question that Bill Dethlefs discussed his diagnosis of my purported mental problem with others in his office and therefore committed a second act of invasion of privacy. However, each of these violations was done with the encouragement of the University, thus it can be viewed as a conspiracy.

In his email of Tuesday, April 16, 2013 to Catie McCorry-Andalis, Associate Vice President and Dean of Students Bill Dethlefs made the statement that I am ". . . having trouble adapting to college life." Since I have maintained an A average since I entered UTEP what did he base his diagnosis on and how have I not adapted?

I did not and do not believe that Bill Dethlefs is legally qualified to make such a diagnosis, or in fact, any diagnosis as he is not licensed by the state to practice psychology or psychiatry and is not a clinical psychologist. He does have a Ph.D. (so he says) in Social work and Psychology, however, this does not automatically make him qualified to diagnose individuals, especially those who do not want to be or are not aware that they are his patients.

The University urges disabled students to come to CASS for assistance in accommodations, not for medical or psychological examinations or diagnosis by someone unqualified to make such determinations. Since the University acts on Dethlefs' off the cuff diagnosis made without the student's knowledge, (at least in my case) this amounts to false pretenses and violates the students' rights again in conjunction with the University administration.

Thus we have an improper, secret diagnosis made after literally no examination of any sort by a man who is not legally qualified to do so. He also stated in his email of April 18, 2013 to Ryan C. Holmes that I (referring to me) "*claim* to have written several books and earned a B.A. and M.A. in Criminal Justice and a JD in Law."

First off, this man who would diagnose me cannot even get his facts straight. He could have seen copies of some of the books I have written by walking down or calling to the UTEP Bookstore or even gone on line and checked out Amazon.

Next I never claimed to have a B.A. and an M.A. in Criminal Justice. I have a B.S. and a M.S. in Criminal Justice as well as a J.D. from an accredited law school. I also lack two classes to have a second Master's Degree which is in Public Administration. So I must ask again where is the *"inability to fit into college life and upon what did he base such a diagnosis?"*

As to him making what amounts to a psychological diagnosis, without either having met the state qualifications to be licensed to make such diagnosis or obtaining my permission or following any of the clinical protocols for making such an improper and probably illegal diagnosis of a perceived disability that has negatively impacted my college career and disseminating to people in authority this diagnosis is a violation of my right to privacy and due process of law as a minimum. In arriving at his diagnosis is it clear he never looked at my medical records or even my educational records as can be shown by the incorrect information he reported about me in emails he sent to those higher in the chain at UTEP. He is also practicing medicine without a license with the support of the University.

The information he reported to higher authorities is either incorrect or taken out of context such as the email of April 16, 2013 when he spoke of "based on his conversations with me, I had had run in with Ben Flores and Yvonne Lopez in the Graduate School and with Dean Witherspoon[129]. . ... He does have a strong personality and is having trouble adapting to college life."

This diagnosis by Bill Dethlefs, that has never been questioned by the University or confirmed by anyone legally competent to make such a diagnosis, violated my rights under the Americans with Disability Act (ADA). This improper diagnosis created a perceived disability in the mind of those in the administration in a manner similar to that outlined in **Wilson v. Phoenix Specialty Mfg. Co.**, Inc., 513 F. 3d 378 - Court of Appeals, 4th Circuit 2008) since now UTEP views my "inability to fit into college life" as a real disability from which I suffer.

In Bill Dethlefs' email of April 18, 2013 to Ryan C. Holmes he says *"I believe there will be more problems until, and if, he can settle into a routine. You don't need to do anything right now. However, I do expect him to be referred to your office at some point in the near future."*

---

[129] It was Dean Witherspoon who said that my Communications Degree (my 5th degree) from her department no less was not much of a degree.

As proof that those to whom Bill Dethlefs communicated his improper diagnosis are swayed by his findings the subject line of an email sent by Ryan C. Holmes to Bill Dethlefs reads "**RE: Student Veteran – Difficult Adjustment to Campus Life**." Thus it is clear that Ryan C. Holmes, as a minimum, viewed me as having a perceived disability as a result of Bill Dethlefs' emails.

It is my belief that by making the improper, false diagnosis and then communicating this false diagnosis to others Bill Dethlefs also violated the rules of privacy under the Health Insurance Portability and Accountability Act of 1996 (HIPPA). UTEP contains a nursing school and a physical therapy school and thus as an institution is bound by HIPPA. For Bill Dethlefs to assume the mantle of a clinical psychologist without state licensure, make a diagnosis without following established protocols and then transmit said diagnosis to others without permission of the unknowing patient is a direct violation of HIPAA. Even worse, except for the filing of a Texas Public Information Act request it would have all remained secret never known by the subject of the emails.

The most egregious part of this matter is that these activities are condoned and encouraged by the highest authority at UTEP as shown by the email from Catie

McCorry-Andalis, dated April 16, 2013, wherein she said
to Bill Dethlefs in regard to his reports on me "you are
doing a great job." Therefore, she was encouraging his
violations of HIPAA and his practicing medicine without a
license and turning the CASS office into an unlicensed
medical facility to, in effect, spy on the disabled.

As for the reports of Maria Michel and Maria
Contreras that were included in the file that make me out to
be a danger, neither report is true and both are defamatory
and I never had the opportunity to respond to them. I have
never laid eyes, to my knowledge on Maria Contreras and
Maria Michel is not reporting what actually happened but
what Ryan C. Holmes wanted her to say. Both also reported
this so called incident only when asked to do so by Ryan C.
Holmes well after the fact.

As part of the Mediation Agreement dated August
20, 2013, (Exhibit A), upon my insistence, I was permitted
to request a file regarding myself in the possession of Ryan
Holmes, Associate Dean of Students, Director of Student
Conduct and Conflict Resolution at the University of Texas
at El Paso (UTEP). The contents of the file make it very
clear that I have been thoroughly monitored by the
University and the violations of my rights went much
further than I was aware of at the time of the mediation. So

I was called in by the official in charge of discipline and asked if I was a danger to myself or others. All of these "findings" were based on my hat which said proud to have served.

I sued the University in State Court based on what had happened. They were represented by the Office of the Attorney General of Texas Greg Abbott, now governor of Texas was the Attorney General at the time. The Assistant Attorney General moved the case to Federal Court and then claimed that the Federal Court had no jurisdiction and asked for dismissal.

The case went before Judge David C. Guaderrama. What was some of the evidence used against me[130] were none other than documents submitted by the State Bar of Georgia that I had been disbarred. I objected to these documents being made a part of the record and as usual was ignored. After all, I was a disbarred lawyer and had no rights in his court. His reputation as a state court judge was that once he made up his mind and nothing could change it. Nothing he did was fair or impartial.

After some other legal shenanigans conducted by the Office of the Attorney General of the State of Texas as well as extensive ex-parte communications between the

---

[130] Not to defend the University, but rather to impeach me.

office of the State Attorney General and the Judge (and, I discovered, UTEP President Natalicio), the case was dismissed. He agreed that he had no jurisdiction.

Had he applied the law, instead of using judicial discretion, remand back to state court was the proper course of action. I entered this action with the belief that I was entitled to at least due process of law, but there was not even a pretense that this was offered by the Court. From a reading of the law, it seems clear that the dismissal by the Judge was improper.

A reading of 28 U.S.C. 1447(c) makes it crystal clear that a remand was the proper action to take since the Defendants specifically raised lack of subject matter jurisdiction as a defense.

Under the provisions of 28 U.S.C., Section 1447(c), the section reads, to wit:

(c) A motion to remand the case on the basis of any defect other than lack of subject matter jurisdiction must be made within 30 days after the filing of the notice of removal under section 1446(a). If at any time before final judgment it appears that the district court lacks subject matter jurisdiction, the case shall be remanded. An order remanding the case may require payment of just costs and any actual expenses, including

attorney fees, incurred as a result of the removal. A certified copy of the order of remand shall be mailed by the clerk to the clerk of the State court. The State court may thereupon proceed with such case.

On page 5 of the Order to Dismiss, the Court states: "When the defendant makes a factual attack by providing affidavits, testimony and other evidence challenging the court's jurisdiction, the plaintiff must submit facts in support of the court's jurisdiction and thereafter bear the burden of proving that the trial court has subject matter jurisdiction. (See Middle S. Energy, Inc. v. City of New Orleans, 800 F. 2nd 488, 490 (5th Cir. 1986).

Frankly, I agreed the Court did not have subject matter jurisdiction and asked the Court for remand (11/14/2013 & 11/20/2013) back to the state court several times under the provisions of 28 U.S.C., Section 1447(c) but each and every time, the Court not only failed to respond to my submissions, but completely ignored my filings.

I received my answer as to what really happened when I ran into Maria Contreras in the hallway. She sneered and literally spat at me. "*Bet you're not so big now*

are you. It took only one call from President Natalico[131]
to the Judge for your case to be dismissed."

Based on this I filed a complaint against the Judge, but as I expected the other Judge's protected him. I was given to understand by the 5th Circuit that one does not make allegations against someone so blessed as a federal judge.

---

[131] She is the University President and God's gift to education, just ask her.

CHAPTER ELEVEN
EPILOGUE

Well, it has been a long and involved story. The State Bar of Georgia using an administrative rule and going before what amounts to a kangaroo court stripped me of my right to practice law, my Constitution Rights and my right to due process of law.

This ruling by a court which had no jurisdiction has been protected by every judge I have tried to get it in front of, both State and Federal. When I have submitted proof of forgery, it has been ignored with the comment "**Why Would They Say It If It Wasn't True**?" Religious fanatics do not protect the word of God as fanatically as courts have protected what the State Bar of Georgia has done to me.

In 25 years I have not had a single meaningful hearing. In New Mexico there was outright bribery involved and favors were called in to ensure that the interests of the State Bar of Georgia were protected.

154\ KEN HUDNALL

The general attitude of every attorney and Judge I went to for help seemed to be you probably did something else, so to hell with you.

The few attorneys who did try to help me were threatened with disbarment as was one Judge in New Mexico. He had started to ask questions that were making some people uncomfortable and was told if did not shut up, he would be framed for drug possession and taken off the bench.

I have made every possible effort to get justice. I worked for a company that became involved in a federal criminal case. The FBI served a subpoena duces tecum and took control of tens of thousands of documents, so many they were having trouble sorting them out. I was asked to assist. I agreed to do so if they would have the so called resignation reviewed by a handwriting expert. The agent, Steve Chambers agreed. He ran the plan by Debra Kanof, an Assistant U.S. Attorney in El Paso handling the criminal case. Instead of allowing him to conduct his case, his way, she snapped at him.

"We are the U.S. Attorney's Office we do not make deals we give orders and by God they better be carried out!"

I later asked him to request that the Atlanta Field Office conduct an investigation into the continued theft of property from Black clients that I am told is still going on. The office refused, stating *"these are fine upstanding members of the Bar, we are not going to investigate them."*

The statute in question allows me to insist on an investigation if I can show proof of violations of the law. I asked the local Federal Judge, Judge David Briones, for an order instructing them to investigate. In spite of the federal law on the matter, under judicial discretion, he refused. The law be damned.

I should not have been surprised since there was a grand jury indictment handed down involving 168 people in this town. When it was released, Attorney General Holder ordered it to be quashed since *"There are too many good democrats on it!"*

All I have ever asked is for what the U.S. Constitution entitled me to have, my day in court. But I guess our legal system is more concerned with the rights of potential terrorists or where someone goes to the bathroom or what they eat for lunch at school than they are with the complete violation of someone's rights. I hope when soldiers are needed again to defend the rights of these dilatants, the soldiers tell them that it is their turn to go risk their lives since they love the illegal immigrants so much. I for one are disgusted after 25 years of asking just for what the law entitles me to have and having that denied to me. I was basically removed from practice on the say so of a State Supreme Court Justice who acted on the recommendation of the Office of General Counsel of the State Bar. Why was I and am I not entitled to a trial if I did something wrong? What are they afraid of?

IN CLOSING: The U.S. Supreme Court has held:

"The assertion of federal rights, when plainly and reasonably made, is not to be defeated under the name of local practice." **Davis v Wechsler**, 263 U.S. 22, 24 (1923)

"Where rights secured by the Constitution are involved, there can be no rule making or legislation which would abrogate them." **Miranda v Arizona**, 384 U.S. 426, 491 (1966)

Due process in the taking of property by any arm of the State is a civil right guaranteed by Section One of the 14th Amendment of the Constitution. Conspiracy to deny due process is a federal felony prosecutable under 18 USC 241. Denial of due process under color of law is a federal misdemeanor under 18 USC 242.

The Director of the Federal Bureau of Investigation is **REQUIRED** by **28 CFR 0.85** to investigate violations of 18 USC 241 and 18 USC 242[132].

THE F.B.I. HAS ALWAYS TURNED ITS BACK ON ME – TOO MANY GOOD DEMOCRATS MIGHT GET HURT.

WHAT PROTECTS THESE LAW BREAKERS? JUDICIAL DISCRETION – THIS TRUMPS THE LAW OF THE LAND[133]!

---

[132] In the face of the statute, Judge David Briones, senior Federal Judge in El Paso, Texas decided under his judicial discretion that the FBI should not be bothered by my little problem. After all, I was just a disbarred attorney, not worth listening too.

[133] *This is a final footnote with two very important facts. (1) I could never find out how the State Bar of Georgia was able to keep such good track of me over the years. I discovered that my step-mother was best friends with Cartledge. She and her first husband were members of the Big Eddy Club along with Cartledge and Judge Land. She told me that she informed Cartledge, who could not be guilty of anything she swore, where I was living and where I worked.*

(2) When Senator Jeff Sessions was approved as U.S. Attorney General, I was informed to not expect any help from him since he was known to have had dinner several times at the Big Eddy Club from time to time and as a result was at worst an ally of those who were running this game. This ill gotten money is known to have funded several political campaigns, I know at least one Democratic congressman who was funded from this slush fund.

EXHIBIT A

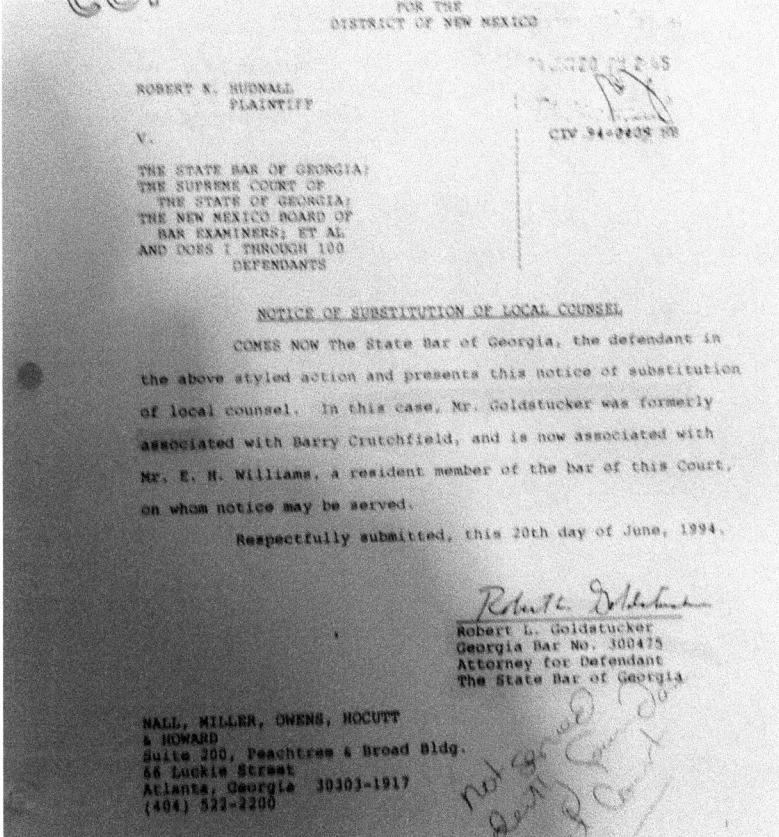

Figure 1: This Notice of Appearance shows that C. Barry Crutchfield had been Georgia's Attorney in New Mexico until June 20, 1994.

EXHIBIT B

Board of Bar Examiners

AN AGENCY OF THE SUPREME COURT
ROSE MARIE ALDERETE
SECRETARY
P.O. BOX 846
SANTA FE, NEW MEXICO 87502

State of New Mexico

REPLY TO:

BARRY CRUTCHFIELD
[illegible] 113 [illegible]
LOVINGTON NEW MEXICO 88260   Washington
396 4937

April 14, 1994

Mr. William P. Smith, III
State Bar of Georgia
50 Hurt Plaza S.E.
Atlanta, Ga

RE: Request For Local Counsel

Dear Mr. Smith:

I was pleased to hear from you yesterday. I was also very comforted to find out that you fully support Paul Cohen's request to me regarding Mr. Hudnall.

As I told Mr. Cohen, in his application Mr. Hudnall has raised some serious claims regarding violation of his right to due process by your office. While Mr. Cohen did confirm that most of Mr. Hudnall's claims are accurate, I fully understand and concur with what was done based upon his reasoning. Unfortunately, such claims, if confirmed, might cause the Panel to vote to waive the good standing rule and admit him here. Even so, I believe that in my dual role of investigator and chair of the Panel, I can have a direct impact on how the Board and the Supreme Court handle his application.

Additionally, after due consideration, I have decided that the "incentive" offered is more than adequate. I will make every effort to keep you up to date on what is taking place, however, I warn you it would not be wise for my affiliation with your office to be known. I look forward to hearing from you.

Sincerely,

C. Barry Crutchfield

Mr. Hudnall
For your info.

Carl C.

Figure 2: Letter from Barry Crutchfield to William P. Smith III

Board of Bar Examiners   State of New Mexico

AN AGENCY OF THE SUPREME COURT
ROSE MARIE ALDERETE
SECRETARY
P.O. BOX 249
SANTA FE, NEW MEXICO 87503

REPLY TO

BARRY CRUTCHFIELD
LOVINGTON, NEW MEXICO   113 East
    Washington

April 4, 1994

Mr. Robert Kenneth Hudnall
721 5th Avenue, #35-C
New York, NY 10022

Re: Application for Admission to New Mexico Bar

Dear Mr. Hudnall:

I have been assigned to review the matters of your application for membership in the New Mexico Bar. As you have been notified, our rules require you to be in "good standing" in any Bar of which you are a member in order to be admitted to practice in New Mexico.

In this regard, I have reviewed the materials you have submitted in connection with your application. Although the matter is somewhat confusing in that I do not have a clear statement of the claims of the State Bar of Georgia, I am troubled by some of the specifics of this matter.

In order that I may have a full and complete understanding of the matter in Georgia, please call me at the number shown above. If I am not in the office, let me know what time is good for your schedule so I may call you. In addition, I am unclear if you have counsel in regard to the matter in Georgia. If so, I will appreciate being advised of such counsel's name, address and phone number.

I look forward to hearing from you in this matter.

Sincerely,

Barry Crutchfield

CDC/nye
xc/   Ms. Rose Marie Alderete

EXHIBIT
D

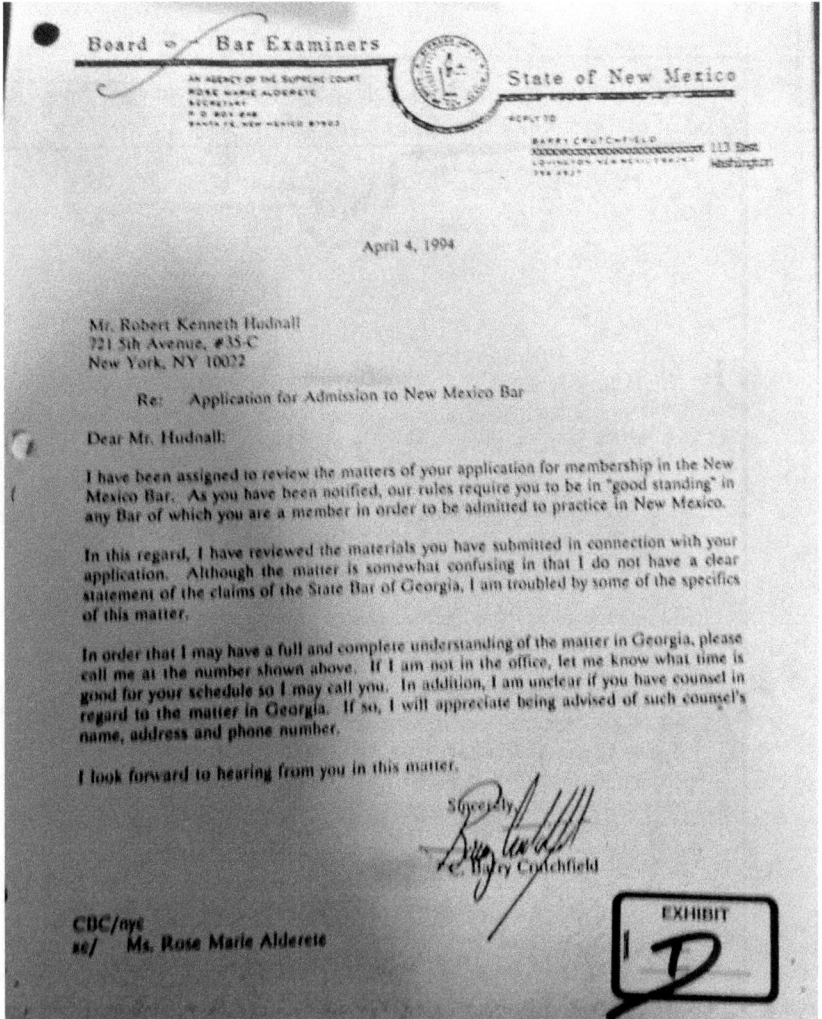

Figure 3: Another letter for comparison of signatures.

EXHIBIT C

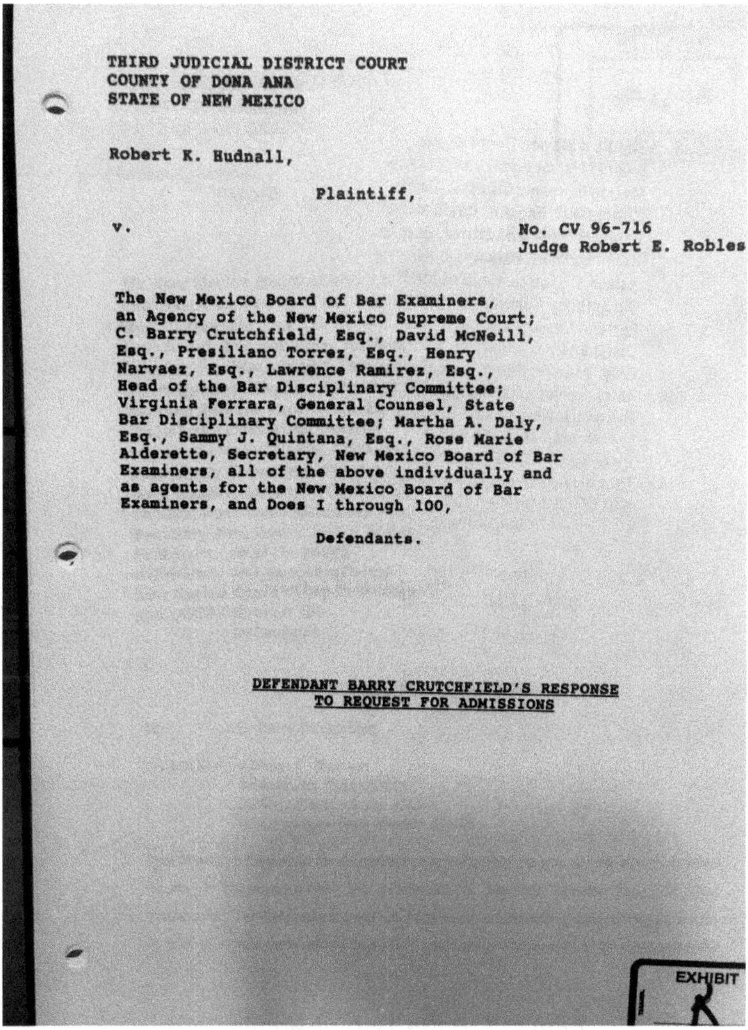

THIRD JUDICIAL DISTRICT COURT
COUNTY OF DONA ANA
STATE OF NEW MEXICO

Robert K. Hudnall,

                    Plaintiff,

v.   No. CV 96-716
                                            Judge Robert E. Robles

The New Mexico Board of Bar Examiners,
an Agency of the New Mexico Supreme Court;
C. Barry Crutchfield, Esq., David McNeill,
Esq., Presiliano Torrez, Esq., Henry
Narvaez, Esq., Lawrence Ramirez, Esq.,
Head of the Bar Disciplinary Committee;
Virginia Ferrara, General Counsel, State
Bar Disciplinary Committee; Martha A. Daly,
Esq., Sammy J. Quintana, Esq., Rose Marie
Alderette, Secretary, New Mexico Board of Bar
Examiners, all of the above individually and
as agents for the New Mexico Board of Bar
Examiners, and Does I through 100,

                    Defendants.

                    DEFENDANT BARRY CRUTCHFIELD'S RESPONSE
                        TO REQUEST FOR ADMISSIONS

EXHIBIT

Figure 4: C. Barry Crutchfield's Admissions

THIRD JUDICIAL DISTRICT COURT
COUNTY OF DONA ANA
STATE OF NEW MEXICO

Robert K. Hudnall
    Plaintiff

v.

The New Mexico Board of Bar
Examiners, an Agency of the New
Mexico Supreme Court; C. Barry
Crutchfield, Esquire; David McNeill,
Esquire; Presiliano Torrez, Esquire;
Henry Narvaez, Esquire; Lawrence
Ramirez, Esquire, Head of the Bar
Disciplinary Committee; Virginia
Ferrara, General Counsel, State Bar
Disciplinary Committee; Martha A.
Daly, Esquire; Sammy J. Quintana,
Esquire; Rose Marie Alderette,
Secretary, New Mexico Board of Bar
Examiners, all of the above
individually and as agents for the
New Mexico Board of Bar Examiners
and DOES 1 through 100
    Defendants

No. CV 96-716
Judge Robert E. Robles

REQUEST FOR ADMISSIONS

TO: C. Barry Crutchfield

THROUGH: William F. Riordan
    Attorney for Defendants
    20 First Plaza - Suite 402
    Albuquerque, New Mexico 87102

The following Requests for Admission are submitted to you in the above entitled cause, in accordance with the provisions of the New Mexico Rules of Civil procedure. The Requests for Admissions shall be answered separately and fully in writing, under oath, within thirty (30) days after the service of the Requests for

1

Figure 5: Page Two of Admissions

Admission. Your answers, to the extent possible, should be placed in the space provided following each Interrogatory.

Demand is made for supplementation of your answers to these Interrogatories as is required by the New Mexico Rules of Civil Procedure.

As to any Request for Production for Examination, Inspection, and Copying of Tangible materials, you are requested to produce and permit the party making this request, or someone acting on such party's behalf, to inspect, test, photograph and/or copy the following documents or tangible things in your possession or under your control, as set forth in the New Mexico Rules of Civil Procedure.

You are requested to produce the items set forth in any Request for Production for Examination, Inspection and Copying of Tangible Materials and make them available for Plaintiff to inspect or copy on or before thirty (30) days following the service of these Interrogatories and Request for Production upon you. If any other time within the time set forth in this request shall be more convenient and any other place shall be more convenient and reasonable for production of the items requested, then you are invited to contact the representative for the party submitting this request in regard to such other more convenient and reasonable time and place for production of the items requested.

Respectfully Submitted,

BY

ROBERT K. HUDNALL, PRO SE
P.O. Box 7947
Las Cruces, New Mexico 88006

A copy of the above and foregoing Interrogatories and Request for Production was this 24th day of September, 1996, furnished to Defendant herein by forwarding same to the attorney of record for Defendant.

2

Figure 6: Page 3 of Admissions

1. Please admit that you were appointed by the New Mexico Board of Bar Examiners to be an investigator into Plaintiff's Application for Admission.

Admit that I was charged with obtaining facts and information concerning Plaintiff's eligibility to be admitted to practice.

2. Please admit that Plaintiff informed you that the resignation being used by the State Bar of Georgia to justify removing Plaintiff from good standing was a forgery.

Admit that Plaintiff alleged that the signature was a forgery, but deny that Plaintiff provided credible proof that the signature was a forgery, and deny that the reasons for Plaintiff's lack of good standing before the Georgia Bar were relevant to his eligibility for admission in New Mexico.

3. Please admit that Plaintiff did furnish you with documentary evidence supporting the premise that his signature on the resignation in question was a forgery.

Deny. Plaintiff provided a document from Paul Osborn that no definite conclusion could be made regarding validity of signature.

4. Please admit that Plaintiff did furnish you with a copy of a handwriting report prepared by Paul Osborn that called into question Plaintiff's signature.

Admit.

5. Please admit that Plaintiff did ask you to look into the matter of the alleged forged resignation in Georgia.

Admit.

6. Please admit that Plaintiff discussed the federal suit with you prior to it being filed.

Admit. Plaintiff indicated that he was preparing litigation against the Georgia Supreme Court.

Figure 7: Page 4 of Admissions

1. Please admit that you were appointed by the New Mexico Board of Bar Examiners to be an investigator into Plaintiff's Application for Admission.

   Admit that I was charged with obtaining facts and information concerning Plaintiff's eligibility to be admitted to practice.

2. Please admit that Plaintiff informed you that the resignation being used by the State Bar of Georgia to justify removing Plaintiff from good standing was a forgery.

   Admit that Plaintiff alleged that the signature was a forgery, but deny that Plaintiff provided credible proof that the signature was a forgery, and deny that the reasons for Plaintiff's lack of good standing before the Georgia Bar were relevant to his eligibility for admission in New Mexico.

3. Please admit that Plaintiff did furnish you with documentary evidence supporting the premise that his signature on the resignation in question was a forgery.

   Deny. Plaintiff provided a document from Paul Osborn that no definite conclusion could be made regarding validity of signature.

4. Please admit that Plaintiff did furnish you with a copy of a handwriting report prepared by Paul Osborn that called into question Plaintiff's signature.

   Admit.

5. Please admit that Plaintiff did ask you to look into the matter of the alleged forged resignation in Georgia.

   Admit.

6. Please admit that Plaintiff discussed the federal suit with you prior to it being filed.

   Admit. Plaintiff indicated that he was preparing litigation against the Georgia Supreme Court.

Figure 8: Page 5 of Admissions

13. Please admit that after your reclusal, you used information gathered by the Panel to prepare your sworn affidavits for the federal court regarding Plaintiff.

    Admit.

14. Please admit that David McNeill requested you to prepare and submit the sworn affidavits prepared by you and sent to the federal court.

    Deny.

15. Please admit that none of Plaintiff's evidence regarding the forged resignation, submitted to you as investigator for the Panel, was submitted to or considered by the Bar Panel prior to a recommendation being made.

    Deny.

16. Please admit that none of Plaintiff's evidence regarding the forged resignation, submitted to you as investigator for the Panel was submitted to or considered by the State Supreme Court prior to denying Plaintiff's Application for Admission.

    Because I recused myself, I am not aware of what was and was not submitted to the Supreme Court. I do not know what the Court considered in rejecting the application.

17. Please admit that you elected to delete Plaintiff's evidence regarding the forgery from consideration due to your personal doubts regarding the credibility of said evidence.

    Deny.

18. Please admit that you had a duty to be fair and impartial in your role as appointed investigator for the Bar Panel.

    Admit. I have a duty to be fair and impartial in carrying out my duties as a member of the Board of Bar Examiners.

5

Figure 9: Page 6 of Admissions

19. Please admit that you received absolutely no information regarding Plaintiff from the Georgia Bar.

Admit that I received no information directly from the Georgia Bar. I received information from the National Conference of Bar Examiners.

20. Please admit that you performed no duties of an investigative nature in regard to you appointment as investigator for the Bar Panel.

Deny; "investigative nature" is not defined and is susceptible to different meanings.

21. Please admit that you notified no one involved with the Bar Panel or the Plaintiff that you were acting as the local counsel for the Georgia Defendants.

I do not recall, since I served as local counsel for only one week.

22. Please admit that you submitted your own personal recommendation to the Bar Panel that Plaintiff not be admitted.

Deny. I did determine that Plaintiff was not eligible for admission.

23. Please admit that you personally determined what information was submitted to the Bar Panel regarding Plaintiff's Application for Admission.

Deny.

24. Please admit that you suppressed from consideration by the Bar Panel certain information in your possession prior to your reclusal from the Panel.

Deny.

25. Please admit that the recommendation submitted by the Panel was the same one that you recommended.

Admit. I assume that the panel concluded Plaintiff was ineligible inasmuch as the State Bar of Georgia had advised, through the National Conference of Bar Examiners, that Mr. Hudnall was not in good standing in Georgia.

Figure 10: Page 7 of Admissions

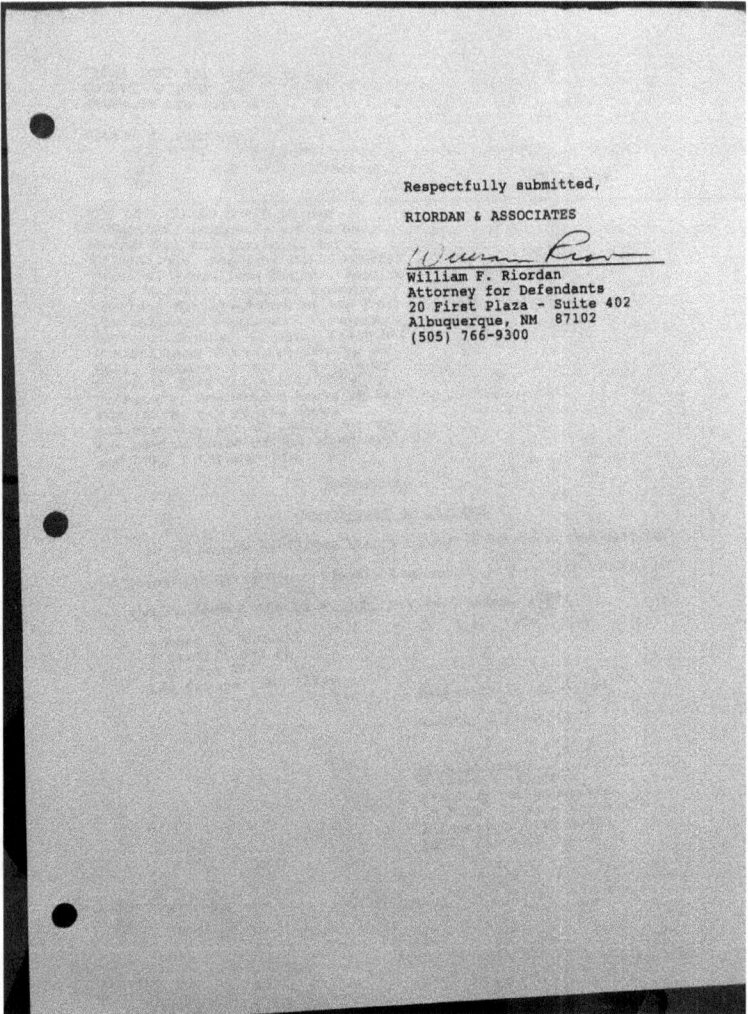

Respectfully submitted,

RIORDAN & ASSOCIATES

William F. Riordan
Attorney for Defendants
20 First Plaza - Suite 402
Albuquerque, NM 87102
(505) 766-9300

Figure 11: Page 8 of Admissions

EXHIBIT D

STATE OF NEW MEXICO

GENERAL SERVICES DEPARTMENT
John F. Simms, Jr. Building
715 Alta Vista, Santa Fe, New Mexico 87503
Mailing Address: P.O. Drawer 26110 • Santa Fe, New Mexico 87502-6110

OFFICE of the SECRETA
(505) 827-2000

ADMINISTRATIVE SERVICES C
(505) 827-2165

BUILDING SERVICES DIVI
(505) 827-2349

INFORMATION SYSTEMS DI
(505) 827-2001

PROPERY CONTROL DIVI
(505) 827-2141

PURCHASING DIVISIO
(505) 827-0472

RISK MANAGEMENT DIVI
(505) 827-0442

GARY E. JOHNSON
GOVERNOR

Steven R. Beffort
SECRETARY

January 23, 1995

Mr. Robert K. Hudnall
P. O. Box 7947
Las Cruces, New Mexico 88006

RE: RMD File No.:   CR/2271BJ
       Insured: State Bar Examiner
       Claimant: Robert K. Hudnall

Dear Mr. Hudnall:

We now have the benefit of your investigation relative to your claim against the State Bar Examiner.

It was found that you were discharged from the Georgia State Bar. The prior disbarment would prevent you from being admitted to practice in New Mexico.

Risk Management Division failed to find any wrong doing on behalf of the State Bar Examiner Board.

Very truly yours,

Betty J. McManaman
Betty J. McManaman
Claims Administrator

BJM/vm

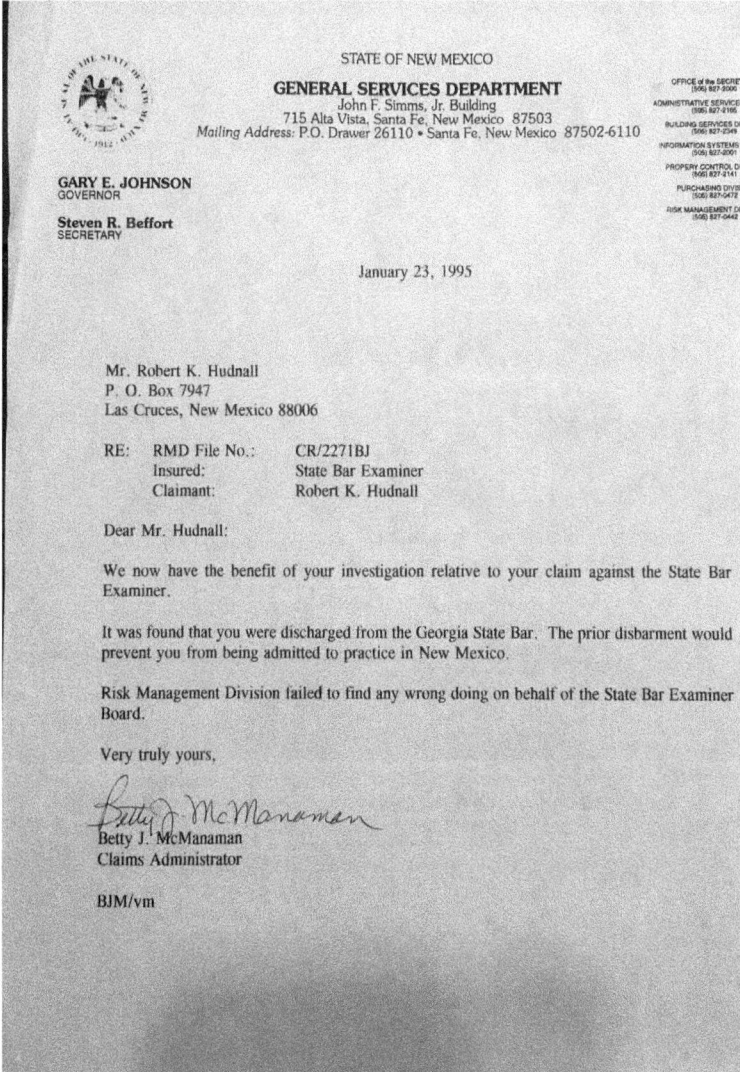

Figure 12: Letter from Betty McManaman that no one did anything wrong.

EXHIBIT E

SUSANA MARTINEZ
NEW MEXICO GOVERNOR

ED BURCKLE
CABINET SECRETARY

State of New Mexico
General Services Department

<u>**VIA E-MAIL**</u>

June 14, 2012

Robert K. Hudnall
5823 N. Mesa #839
El Paso, TX 79912

Re: Request to Inspect Public Records

Dear Mr. Hudnall,

On June 12, the New Mexico General Services Department received your request to inspect public records. You requested:

- Updated "Notice of Suit" received on or about 10/28/1996 from Robert K. Hudnal addressed to Risk Management.
- November 1, 1994 Memorandum to SOARS Investigation to determine the facts, exposure and date of loss.
- January 16, 1996 report from SOARS (Roland Swanson) with attachments.
- Copy of Complaint, correspondence and other documents concerning assignment of the case for defense.

This correspondence is to advise that the records you have requested are dated beyond the 7-year retention schedule required for the Risk Management Division. Thus, we recovered no responsive records.

Please let me know at your earliest convenience if you have questions about our response. Otherwise, we will consider your records request closed.

Sincerely,

Tim Korte
Records Custodian

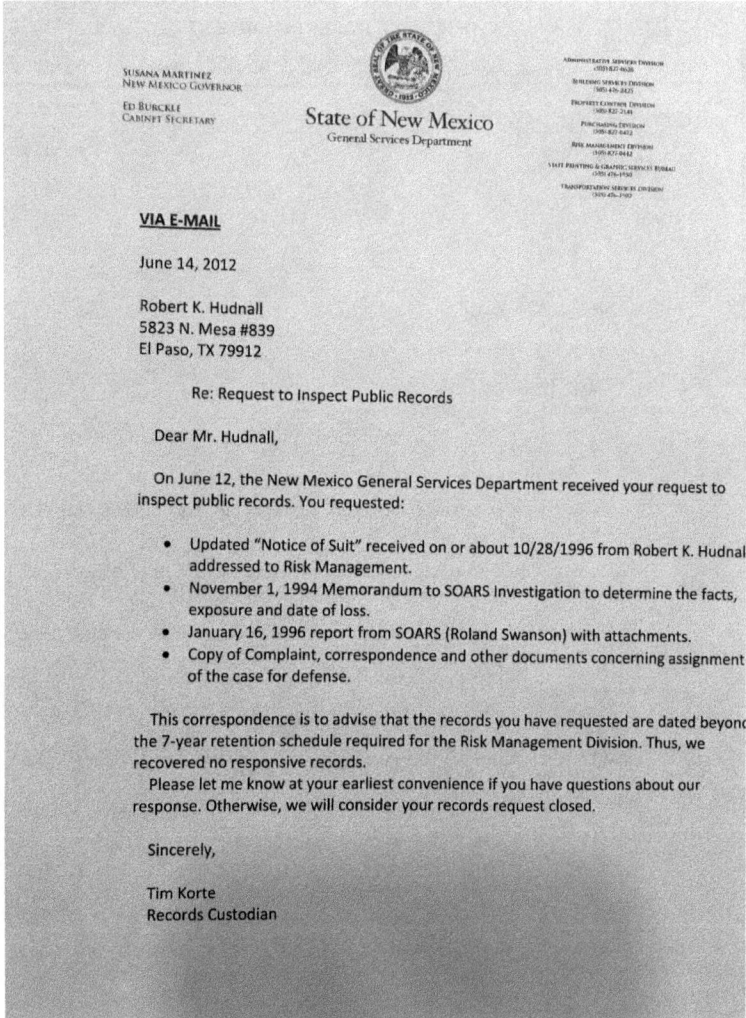

Figure 13: E-mail from Tim Korte that the report had been destroyed.

EXHIBIT F

TIME TABLE

October 1993	Meeting with Lawrence Ramirez regarding taking Bar, with witnesses. Mr. Ramirez said the issue of Georgia wouldn't be a problem if I could pass the bar exam.
November 19, 1993	Submitted Application for Admission
November 22, 1993	Application for Admission received by NM Board of Bar Examiners. (See Exhibit B of Complaint)
November 29, 1993	NM Board of Bar Examiners acknowledged receipt of Plaintiff's application (See Exhibit C of Complaint)
December 1993	National Conference of Bar Examiners conducted investigation.
January 24, 1994	National Conference of Bar Examiners submitted report to New Mexico, which the bar refuses to show to Plaintiff. (See Crutchfield Interrogatories Response to Question 15.)
February 21-23, 1994	Dates of NM Bar Exam (See Exhibit C1 of Complaint)
March 24, 1994	Notification by Rose Marie Alderette that even if Plaintiff passed he would not be admitted. (Exhibit D of Complaint)
April 4, 1994	C. Barry Crutchfield sent letter that he was appointed to review application for admission. (Exhibit E of Complaint)
Prior to April 20, 1994	C. Barry Crutchfield has stated under oath that he had completed his investigation by this time. (See Interrogatory 24 wherein Mr. Crutchfield states that "At the time of the (federal) litigation, (filed 4/20/94) the investigation as to eligibility of Mr. Hudnall was complete.)
April 20, 1994	Federal suit was filed against the Georgia Bar, Georgia Supreme Court and the New Mexico Board of Bar Examiners.

EXHIBIT J

Figure 14: Page 1 of Time Table

May 20, 1994	Word sent from Lawrence Ramirez through Richard Breazell that Plaintiff was to be in New Mexico by June 3, 1994 to be sworn in. (See Affidavit from Richard Breazell)
May 30, 1994	Plaintiff arrived back in New Mexico expecting to be sworn in. Told it had been postponed, but would happen within a week.
June 5-July 29, 1995	Talked numerous times to C. Barry Crutchfield regarding his "thorough" investigation. (See Affidavit of Richard Breazell.)
Prior to June 13, 1994	*C. Barry Crutchfield had completed his investigation and found that Plaintiff was not eligible. (See Interrogatory #10: ". . .I made the decision that Plaintiff was not eligible for admission prior to June 20, 1994.) He Did not tell Plaintiff!!!!!!!*
Prior to June 13, 1994	*C. Barry Crutchfield made his decision and recused himself from case.* (See Interrogatory #14: "By the time I served as local counsel for approximately one week [June 13-20, 1994] in Plaintiff's litigation against the Board of Bar Examiners in United States District Court [he actually represented the Georgia Bar], I had already made my recommendation that Plaintiff was not eligible for admission and had recused.")
June 13-20, 1994	C. Barry Crutchfield served as local counsel for the Georgia Defendants in Plaintiff's case, while allegedly serving as investigator and chair of the panel. (See Defendants' Answer to Paragraph 9 where this is admitted)
June 20, 1994	David McNeill, NM Bar's attorney in the federal case, without any authority, on his firm's stationary, notifies Plaintiff that C. Barry Crutchfield's investigation is

2

Figure 15: Page 2 of Time Table

EXHIBIT G

S94Y05...

SUPREME COURT OF GEORGIA

MAR 1 7 1994

ATLANTA

The Honorable Supreme Court met pursuant to adjournment.

The following order was passed:

IN THE MATTER OF: ROBERT K. HUDNALL

This Court previously accepted Robert K. Hudnall's Petition for Voluntary Surrender of License, and ordered that upon seeking —reinstatement, Hudnall must comply with the reinstatement Rules under Bar Rule 4-301 et. seq. Because Robert K. Hudnall, who directly petitions this Court for reinstatement to the practice of law in Georgia, has failed to follow the reinstatement procedures, this Court refuses to consider his petition and it is hereby dismissed.

SUPREME COURT OF THE STATE OF GEORGIA,

CLERK'S OFFICE, ATLANTA

I certify that the above is a true extract from the minutes of the Supreme Court of Georgia.

Witness my signature and the seal of said court hereto affixed the day and year last above written.

Lynn M. Stinchcomb, Deputy Clerk

EXHIBIT "B"

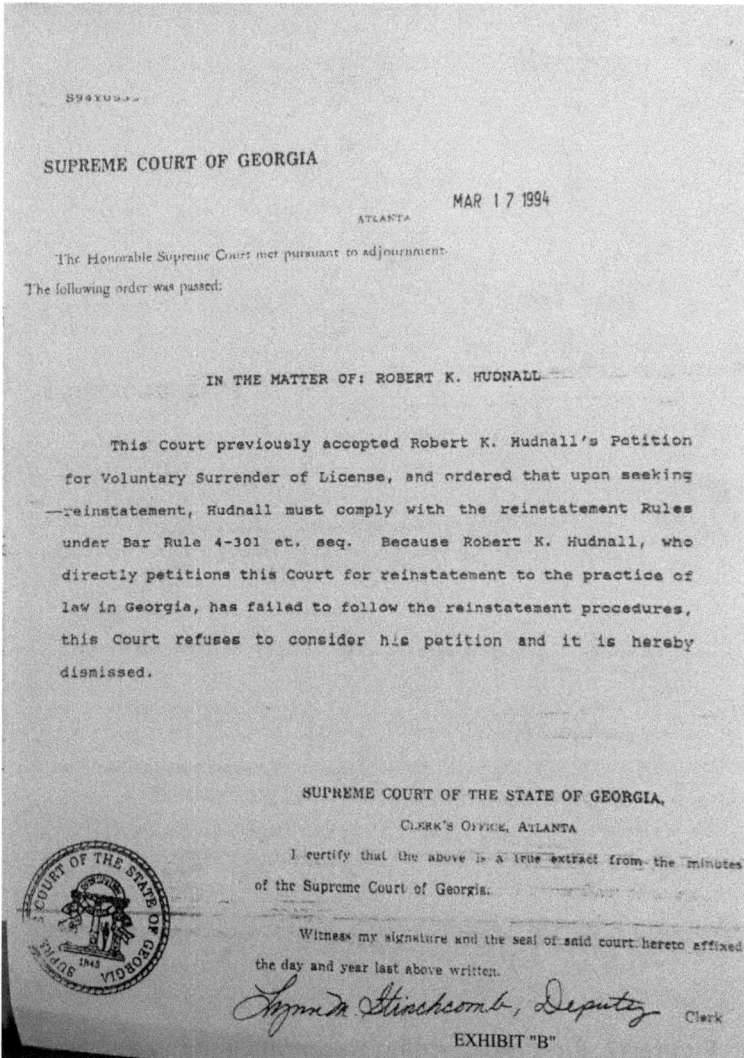

Figure 16: Decision from the Georgia Supreme Court refusing to accept my evidence of forgery.

EXHIBIT H

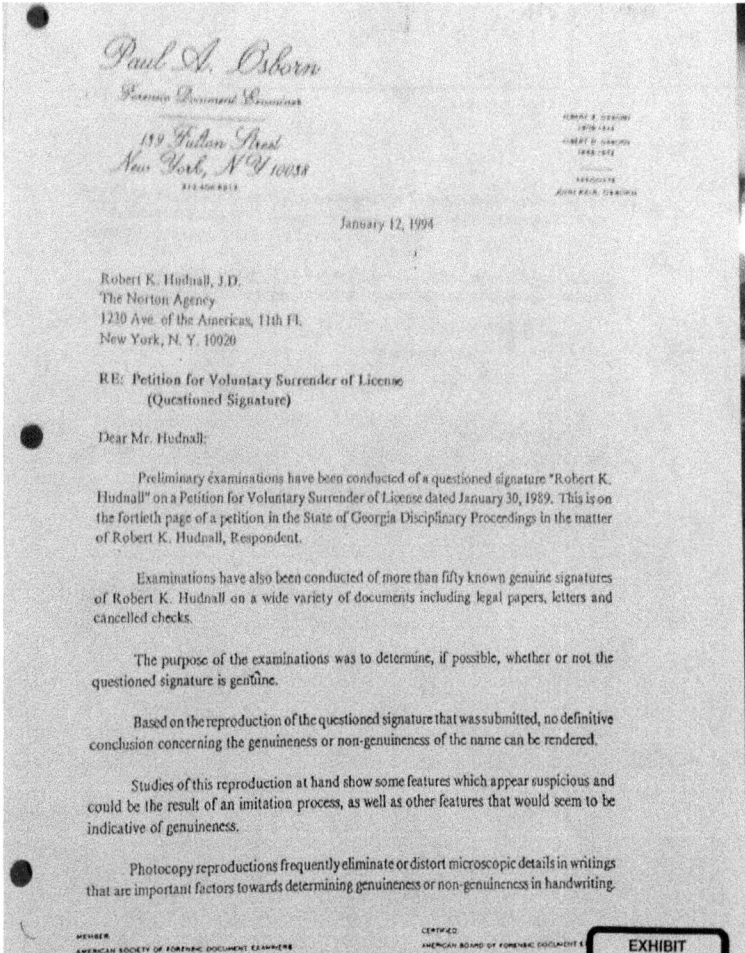

Paul A. Osborn
Forensic Document Examiner

159 Fulton Street
New York, N.Y. 10038

January 12, 1994

Robert K. Hudnall, J.D.
The Norton Agency
1230 Ave. of the Americas, 11th Fl.
New York, N. Y. 10020

RE: Petition for Voluntary Surrender of License
(Questioned Signature)

Dear Mr. Hudnall:

Preliminary examinations have been conducted of a questioned signature "Robert K. Hudnall" on a Petition for Voluntary Surrender of License dated January 30, 1989. This is on the fortieth page of a petition in the State of Georgia Disciplinary Proceedings in the matter of Robert K. Hudnall, Respondent.

Examinations have also been conducted of more than fifty known genuine signatures of Robert K. Hudnall on a wide variety of documents including legal papers, letters and cancelled checks.

The purpose of the examinations was to determine, if possible, whether or not the questioned signature is genuine.

Based on the reproduction of the questioned signature that was submitted, no definitive conclusion concerning the genuineness or non-genuineness of the name can be rendered.

Studies of this reproduction at hand show some features which appear suspicious and could be the result of an imitation process, as well as other features that would seem to be indicative of genuineness.

Photocopy reproductions frequently eliminate or distort microscopic details in writings that are important factors towards determining genuineness or non-genuineness in handwriting.

MEMBER
AMERICAN SOCIETY OF FORENSIC DOCUMENT EXAMINERS

CERTIFIED
AMERICAN BOARD OF FORENSIC DOCUMENT E

EXHIBIT

Figure 17: First Handwriting Report calling the signature into question.

Robert K. Hudnall, J.D.
The Norton Agency
January 12, 1994 - Page 2

It must also be kept in mind that it is realitively easy for one to prepare a photocopy of a non-existant original (signed) document, but showing a reproduction of a genuine signature (which had originally been written for some other purpose).

These are the reasons why it is of real importance that an opportunity be made to examine and photograph the original questioned signature before any conclusions are rendered as to its validity.

Yours respectfully,

PAO/ms

QUALIFICATIONS OF PAUL A. OSBORN

Paul A. Osborn is a Forensic Document Examiner, commonly termed a handwriting and typewriting identification expert, and maintains offices in New York City. He has been qualified as an expert and has testified on the subject of disputed documents in civil and criminal courts on more than four hundred and fifty occasions in the states of New York, New Jersey, Pennsylvania, Massachusetts and seventeen other states, as well as in the Panama Canal Zone, Virgin Islands and Canada.

He has studied the leading books on the subject, collected reference material, conducted numerous experiments and, in fact, has devoted all his time to the investigation of disputed documents since 1953. This includes the identification of handwriting, typewriting, inks, paper, writing instruments, photocopiers, determining the sequence of writing, showing obliterations and erasures and other questions related to documents. He has files of all the national systems of handwriting as well as many foreign systems, maintains up-to-date records of all makes and models of typewriters and printers, keeps periodic specimens of various inks, has annual records of all paper manufacturers and a good deal of other reference material.

He is presently associated with his son, John Paul Osborn, and was associated with his father, Albert D. Osborn, for nineteen years. He was also associated with Francis D. Murphy for four years, who was previously the document examiner for the New York City Police Laboratory.

As part of his training for this work, he took a course of study over a period of three and a half years under the direction of the American Society of Questioned Document Examiners. He is presently an active member and served as the Society's President from 1990 to 1992. Mr. Osborn is also a Fellow of the American Academy of Forensic Sciences (former Section Chairman). He is certified by the American Board of Forensic Document Examiners, Inc.

He has all of the necessary equipment and instruments used in this work, including different types of magnifiers, microscopes, measuring plates, lighting instruments, projectors, infrared and ultraviolet light outfits, a variety of cameras and photographic equipment, electrostatic detection apparatus, video spectral comparator and other instruments.

Mr. Osborn did this work a number of years for the State Police of New Jersey and frequently does work for district attorneys' offices in New York. He has lectured on the subject many times, to groups at Indiana University, the New York Law School and Brooklyn Law School, as well as many banking and bar associations.

A number of articles written by Mr. Osborn have been published in leading forensic journals.

EXHIBIT I

Susan E. Abbey
Board Certified Document Examiner

Phone: (214) 343-1874 Voice Mail: (214) 395-6140
www.handwritingexpert.com

June 17, 2015

TO: Richard Deck
   Attorney at Law
   521 Texas Avenue
   El Paso, Texas 79901

REQUEST: To examine the signature of Ken Hudnall on a document to determine if it is genuine.

DOCUMENTS EXAMINED:

QUESTIONED DOCUMENT:

Q- Copy of Respondent's page dated 1/30/89.

KNOWN EXEMPLARS BEARING THE SIGNATURES OF ROBERT K. HUDNALL:

K1- Copy of letter to Peter C. Quezada dated 4/10/86.
K2- Copy of page to letter stating "I am sorry if this...." undated.
K3- Copy of Affidavit dated 1/10/94.

Copies of the documents listed above are attached to this report.

OPINION:

Based on the documents provided, I am inconclusive as to the authenticity of the signature. My opinion about the signature is limited due to only being able to look at copies, the quality of the questioned copies and some of the known documents provided, as well as the natural variation in the known writings of Mr. Hudnall. Even if I had additional known documents, the quality of the copy of the document in question does not allow the ability to discern between a genuine and non-genuine signature. Additionally, signatures can be "cut and pasted" to documents without evidence being left behind. "Cut and paste" is a term used to describe the affixation of material from one document to another.

My opinions follow the ASTM guidelines for Standard Terminology in Expressing Conclusions of Forensic Document Examiners. My opinions are based upon the examination of the documents reviewed and I reserve the right to amend my opinions should I receive additional information, documents or original documents.

EXHIBIT C

Figure 18: Second handwriting report calling the signature into question.

METHODOLOGY:

Various magnifiers, measuring devices, and enlargements were used to carefully compare the known documents to the questioned documents in accordance with generally accepted document examination guidelines and principles as outlined by ASTM standard #2290 – Standard Guide for Examination of Handwritten Items, and ASTM standard #E2331-04 Standard Guide for Examination of Altered Documents.

STATEMENT OF QUALIFICATIONS:

Attached hereto is a copy of my current curriculum vitae which outlines my background and experience to undertake this examination and render an opinion. Also attached hereto is a signed Certificate of Report.

CONCLUDING REMARKS:

If asked to do so, I am willing to testify under oath in a legal proceeding that all statements and representations made in this report are true and accurate to the best of my knowledge and belief, and I would be prepared to demonstrate and explain the reasons expressed for the opinion given. If court testimony is required, I would prepare appropriate court exhibits to illustrate and explain my findings and opinion.

Respectfully submitted,

Susan E. Abbey, CDE, D-BFDE
Forensic Document Examiner

CERTIFICATE OF REPORT

The undersigned hereby certifies that, except as otherwise noted in the report to which this certificate is attached:

1. I have no present or prospective interest in the subject of the Report, or in the use of the report.

2. I have no personal acquaintance, knowledge, interest or bias with respect to the parties mentioned in the Report.

3. To the best of my knowledge and belief, the statements of facts contained in the Report, upon which the analysis, opinion, and conclusions expressed in the report, are based on the evidence presented to me, are true, correct and reliable to the best of my knowledge.

4. The analysis, opinions and conclusions set forth in the Report are my personal, unbiased professional analysis, opinions, and conclusions and are limited only by the reported assumptions and limiting conditions set forth in the Report.

5. No one other than the undersigned prepared the analysis, conclusions, and opinions concerning the documents that are set forth in the Report.

6. My compensation is not contingent on an action or event resulting from the analysis, opinion, or conclusions in, or the use of the Report.

By: _____

Susan E. Abbey, D-BFDE, CDE
Forensic Document Examiner

Susan E. Abbey
Board Certified Document Examiner

Phone: (214) 343-1874   Voice Mail: (214) 395-6140
www.handwritingexpert.com

CURRICULUM VITAE

*Specializing in: Scientific Examination of Questioned Documents/Handwriting,
Alterations of Documents, Anonymous Notes, Disguised Writing, Desktop
Forgery (Computer/Copier/Printer/Fax), Forged/Authentic Signatures,
Handwriting/Typewriting Identification, Non-Destructive Ink and Paper Examination*

CERTIFICATIONS:
Diplomate- Board of Forensic Document Examiners. Passed a 240 question cognitive exam
and 8 part performance examination. The BFDE certification process is accredited by the
Forensic Specialties Accreditation Board.
Board Certification by the National Association of Document Examiners (NADE). Passed written
and oral examinations.

COURT QUALIFICATIONS: Susan Abbey has met and been qualified under the Daubert/duPont
guidelines. She has testified as an expert witness one or more times in the following courts:

U. S. District Court for the Northern District of
Texas Dallas Division
U. S. District Court for the Southern District of
Texas Houston Division
U. S. Military Court, Fort Sam Houston, Texas
U. S. Bankruptcy Court for the Northern
District of Texas, Dallas Division
Sebastian County Circuit Court, Fort Smith
District, Civil Division VI Arkansas
Escambia County First Judicial Circuit
Court, Pensacola, Florida
District Court of Comanche County, State of
Oklahoma
Texas:
438th District Court Bexar County
103rd District Court Cameron County
219th District Court Collin County
366th District Court Collin County
298th District Court Dallas County
255th District Court Dallas County
193rd District Court Dallas County
191st District Court Dallas County
160th District Court Dallas County
101st District Court Dallas County
95th District Court Dallas County
44th District Court Dallas County
14th District Court Dallas County

367th District Court Denton County
Dallas County Court of Law No. 3
Dallas County Criminal Court No. 4
Dallas County JP Court Precinct 5, Place 2
Dallas County Probate Court No. 1
Dallas County Probate Court No. 3
Denton County District Court No. 367
Ellis County Court No. 1
171st District Court El Paso County
Grand Prairie Municipal Court No. 2
Harris County Probate Court No. 2
Harris Country District Courts, 184th Criminal
Court
370th District Court Hidalgo County
354th District Court Hunt County
422nd District Court Kaufman County
415th District Court Parker County
Tarrant County Probate Court No. 1
Tarrant County District Court No. 48
Tarrant County District Court No. 96
Tarrant County District Court No.
Tarrant County District Court No. 322
Texas Education Agency SOAH Docket
Wise County Court at Law

Susan Abbey
Curriculum Vitae p.2

COURT APPOINTMENTS:

United States District Court Western District of Texas Pecos Division
County Court No. 2 Collin County, Texas
292nd District Court of Dallas County, Texas
County Court at Law of Houston County, Texas
196th Judicial District Hunt County, Texas
354th Judicial District Hunt County, Texas
216th District Court Kendall County, Texas
19th Judicial District McLennan County, Texas
54th Judicial District McLennan County, Texas
4th Judicial District Rusk County, Texas
36th Judicial District San Patricio County, Texas
114th District Court Smith County, Texas
Tarrant County Criminal Court No. 2
299th Judicial District Travis County, Texas
294th Judicial District Van Zandt County, Texas

EDUCATION:

BA Rice University, Houston, Texas, 1980 Business Management.
Forensic Document Examination Course with the National Questioned Document
Association (a state licensed school) 1996-1997. Certification of Completion issued
1997. (Approximately 250 study hours).
American Institute of Applied Science, Inc. Course in Questioned Documents
Certificate of Completion issued 1997. (Approximately 50 study hours).
Mentored under Katherine Koppenhaver D-BCDE, CDE and Linda James, CDE 1997-1998.

PROFICIENCY TESTING: Collaborative Testing Services 2008, 2010, 2013. All questions answered
correctly.

CONTINUING EDUCATION: **411 total hrs**

April, 2015 SEAK conference on How to Be an Effective Witness	7.5 hrs
April, 2015 NADE Conference, Nashville, Tennessee	35 hrs
October, 2014 AFDE Symposium Salt Lake City, Utah	20.5 hrs
October, 2013 Hooke College of Applied Sciences, Westmont, Illinois	8 hrs
October, 2013 AFDE Symposium, Chicago, Illinois	20.5 hrs
May, 2013 NADE Conference, Omaha, Nebraska	19 hrs
May, 2012 NADE Conference, San Diego, California	19 hrs
November, 2011 AFDE Symposium, Louisville, Kentucky	20.5 hrs
May, 2011 NADE Pre-Conference Theory and Skills IR/UV and Indented Writing Examinations, Montreal, Canada	14 hrs
May, 2011 NADE Conference, Montreal, Canada	19 hrs
May, 2010 NADE Conference, Portland, Oregon	23 hrs
April, 2008 NADE Pre-Conference, Austin, Texas	27 hrs
April, 2008 NADE Conference, Austin, Texas	14 hrs
May, 2007 NADE Pre-Conference, Forensic Photography, Tucson, Arizona	4 hrs
May, 2007 NADE Conference, Tucson, Arizona	25 hrs
May, 2006 NADE Conference, Mariner of Seas, Caribbean Ocean	19 hrs
May, 2003 NADE Conference, New Orleans, Louisiana	20 hrs
March, 2001 NQDA Conference, Dallas, Texas	14 hrs
October, 2000 NADE Conference, Albuquerque, New Mexico	17 hrs
March, 2000 National Questioned Document Association Conference, Dallas	14 hrs
October, 1998 NADE Conference, New Orleans, Louisiana	23 hrs
August, 1997 Seminar by Linda L. Collins, B.C.D.E. and Kay Micklitz	7 hrs

INDEX

www.ingramcontent.com/pod-product-compliance
Lightning Source LLC
Chambersburg PA
CBHW071225210326
41597CB00016B/1952